CRICKET'S GOLDEN CUP

THE FINALS 1972–2002

DEAN P. HAYES

SUTTON PUBLISHING

Sutton Publishing Limited
Phoenix Mill · Thrupp · Stroud
Gloucestershire · GL5 2BU

First published 2003

Copyright © Dean Hayes, 2003

British Library Cataloguing in Publication Data
A catalogue record for this book is available from the British Library.

ISBN 0-7509-3235-X

Typeset in 10.5/13.5 Photina.
Typesetting and origination by
Sutton Publishing Limited.
Printed and bound in England by
J.H. Haynes & Co. Ltd, Sparkford.

Picture Credits

All photographs are from the *Lancashire Evening Post* except:

Gold Award Winners

1972	Chris Balderstone (*Leicester Mercury*)
1988	Steve Jefferies (*The News*, Portsmouth)
1997/2001	Ben Hollioake (*Evening Standard*)
2000	Ian Harvey (*Gloucestershire Echo*)
2002	Ian Bell (*Express & Star*)

Contents

Alec Stewart

Carl Hooper

Paul Smith

John Abrahams

Richard Ellison

Introduction

Launched in 1972, when one-day cricket was in its infancy, the Benson and Hedges Cup was a major highlight of the cricket season for thirty-one years. Though it was the last of this country's four major cricket competitions to arrive on the scene and the only one that was linked to a single sponsor throughout its lifetime, it was also the first to depart.

The Benson and Hedges Cup format was to find four quarter-finalists from four regional groups of five, made up from the seventeen first-class counties, with Cambridge University and Minor Counties (North and South) making the numbers up.

As the years unfolded, the regional theory was abandoned in the interests of fairness. Also during the 1990s, it became a straight knockout. Its 55-over format was reduced to 50, in order to give the game one competition played to standard ICC regulations, and the same fielding restrictions were imposed.

Often, of course, the most memorable moments of the Benson and Hedges Cup occurred in the earlier rounds of the competition. Brian Davison's unbeaten 158 for Leicestershire against Warwickshire was the very first Benson and Hedges century and was scored in the very first season of the competition. In 1974, a young Ian Botham first hit the headlines by hitting the winning runs against Hampshire despite having lost four teeth when hit by a ball from West Indian fast bowler Andy Roberts. Three years later, Gloucestershire's Mike Procter took four wickets in five balls against Hampshire – a feat that was surpassed in 1996 when fellow South African Shaun Pollock took four wickets in four balls for Warwickshire against Leicestershire on what was his debut.

In 1979, Somerset's Brian Rose made the headlines in a group game against Worcestershire by declaring his team's innings with just one run on the board. Somerset deliberately lost the match to go through to the next round on a technicality.

Also that year, Essex won the Benson and Hedges Cup, their first major trophy, and Graham Gooch made 120 in what was at that time the highest score in a final (until two years later, when Viv Richards made 132 not out for Somerset against Surrey). The Essex player also holds the record for the highest score in the competition with 198 not out against Sussex at Hove in 1982.

A year later, Middlesex beat Gloucestershire in the quarter-final on the toss of a coin after their game had been rained-off – this was to lead to the 'bowl-out'.

In 1984, Peter May caused the raising of a few eyebrows when he presented the Gold Award to Lancashire's John Abrahams – who had failed to trouble the scorers and hadn't bowled!

Yorkshire won the 1987 Final against Northamptonshire since, with the scores level, they had lost fewer wickets. The following year saw Hampshire experience their first ever Benson and Hedges Final: they won with 23 overs to spare after Steve Jefferies had taken four wickets for one run in eight balls!

In 1989 Mike Atherton's Combined Universities side almost reached the semi-final. They fell just three runs short of Somerset's total, with England's captain-to-be Nasser Hussain making 118. In the Final that year, Nottinghamshire's Eddie Hemmings hit the last ball of the game from Essex's John Lever for four to clinch an unlikely victory.

Lancashire and Worcestershire contested the next two finals, winning one each before Malcolm Marshall, having missed his side's previous two appearances in one-day finals, helped Hampshire win the trophy for a second time in 1992.

The Cup winners in 1993 and 1994 had come through by winning a 'bowl-out' after each had been involved in a rained-off match. The match between Warwickshire and Kent in 1994 was a most controversial affair in that Kent, who lost the 'bowl-out', were unhappy about the pre-match covering. That year, Warwickshire not only won the Benson and Hedges Cup, but the County Championship and NatWest Trophy as well!

Though Lancashire won in 1995, it was Kent's Sri Lankan batsman Aravinda de Silva who lit up the proceedings with a magnificent innings of 112. Lancashire retained the trophy the following year to become winners for the fourth time, while in 1997, South Africa's Hansie Cronje helped Ireland to their first ever victory over a first-class side when they beat Middlesex. The Final was won by Surrey, for whom Ben Hollioake made 98 – described by *Wisden* as 'an innings of innocent near-genius'. Sadly no longer with us, Hollioake became the only player to win two Gold Awards in Benson and Hedges Cup Finals when he won the award again in 2001. Sandwiched in between Surrey's victories were one for Essex and two for Gloucestershire, who had developed into one of the best ever one-day sides. Finally, the last winners of this magnificent competition were Warwickshire.

No fewer than sixteen counties have won the Benson and Hedges Cup, and I hope this book will bring back many happy memories for the vast majority of cricket followers.

Dean Hayes, Pembrokeshire
February 2003

The Finals

1972

LEICESTERSHIRE v YORKSHIRE

Leicestershire's 93-year search for a major cricket award came to an end when they defeated Yorkshire by five wickets to become the first winners of the Benson and Hedges Cup.

It wasn't the free-scoring spectacular that many had hoped for. Runs were hard to come by with both sides bowling and fielding with genuine aggression. But it was a truly absorbing and intense contest, commanding the sort of atmosphere synonymous with Cup Finals.

Following a week of glorious sunshine, the weather changed for the worse overnight, with heavy downpours of rain. The umpires, David Constant and Tommy Spencer, had to make two inspections before they were able to announce that play would begin on time.

The man who tipped the scales in Leicestershire's favour was Chris Balderstone – a player released from the Yorkshire staff two years earlier. Playing his first ever innings in the competition, Balderstone hit an unbeaten 42 to see Leicestershire home. He duly won the Gold Award as 'Man of the Match' for his had been the first really assured innings of the whole game.

Yorkshire, who were without their skipper Geoff Boycott, lost their first wicket with the score on 17 when Richard Lumb played forward and missed a good length ball and lost his off-stump to the impressive Graham McKenzie. The Australian was putting absolutely everything into extracting an extra bit of pace from the wicket. A fast rising ball almost forced Sharpe to play on but it was to be Higgs who captured his scalp when he edged an outswinger to Roger Tolchard, who took a spectacular catch. New bowler Brian Davison was given a cruel baptism. Leadbeater cut a four and hooked a six off consecutive balls, his first over costing 11 runs.

Leadbeater, who had been hit on the left arm by Spencer early in his spell, left the field briefly and re-appeared with his wrist strapped. McKenzie resumed at the pavilion end and together with Davison

Richard Lumb

Ray Illingworth

succeeded in slowing Yorkshire down even further. After 24 overs, the White Rose county's total was only 59. In the second over of his second spell, McKenzie trapped Hampshire leg-before. After two consecutive maidens, bringing the run rate down to a little over 2 per over, Leadbeater – obviously feeling a good deal of discomfort from his injured left arm – retired from the field to be replaced by John Woodford. It was later announced that Leadbeater had severe bruising to his wrist but it was hoped that he would be able to resume if necessary.

Woodford attempted the first aggressive shot for some time when he tried to sweep Illingworth to square-leg but he got under the ball and lofted a catch to Terry Spencer on the boundary, leaving Yorkshire 65 for 4. Davison became the first Leicestershire bowler to complete his 11-over allocation – his figures were 0 for 22 with eleven of these runs having come from his first over!

Two balls after lunch, Hutton was out when he mistimed an off-drive and was caught by Spencer off the bowling of Steele. It looked as though Steele had taken another wicket in his next over when Chris Old lobbed the ball towards Hayward at mid-wicket. The fielder made a lot of ground and just got to the ball as it fell to the ground. Old was on his way back to the dressing-room but he was called back by Umpire Spencer after the ball had touched

GOLD AWARD WINNER 1972
CHRIS BALDERSTONE

Chris Balderstone was one of an increasingly rare breed of players who successfully combined county cricket with League football.

He began his football career with Huddersfield Town but, despite blossoming under the management of Eddie Boot, he could never be guaranteed a first team place and he was transferred in 1965 to Carlisle United. Nine years later he played in the Cumbrian club's first ever Division One game, going on to score 68 goals in 376 League games before joining Doncaster Rovers. He later ended his football career north of the border with Queen of the South.

Balderstone initially played county cricket for Yorkshire but his career as a right-hand batsman and slow left-arm bowler never really took off. In 1971 he joined Leicestershire and was awarded his county cap two years later. On 15 September 1975, in the middle of an innings for Leicestershire against Derbyshire at Chesterfield, he appeared for Doncaster Rovers against Brentford that evening!

The following year, in the match against Sussex at Eastbourne, just before the final Test against the West Indies (Balderstone had appeared in two Tests; his last at The Oval saw him bowled by Holding in both innings without scoring), he collected 93 in a low-scoring game and with his valuable left-arm spin he took eight wickets, including the hat-trick. That is the sort of performance which made him such a highly rated member of the Leicestershire side, for whom he went on to score over 10,000 runs and take 250 wickets.

His opportunities with Yorkshire were limited, football being so much more the important pursuit that a move almost certainly had to be beneficial to him. The question that cricket followers must ask is how good a player might Balderstone have become had his greater allegiance been to cricket.

the ground. But Old didn't have long to go. He hit a towering four off Steele but in the 41st over, he was adjudged lbw off Illingworth when going for another big hit.

Yorkshire were saved from what might have been an embarrassingly low total by a bustling stand between Colin Johnson and David Bairstow, who added 30 runs in the space of eight overs. The last ten overs, normally the most costly time in one-day matches, passed by with 32 extra runs put on and when the innings closed, Tony Nicholson and Howard Cooper were still there, denying Leicestershire the distinction of having bowled the opposition out in every round of the competition.

Having reduced Yorkshire to 136 for 9, Leicestershire were expected to keep up comfortably with the winning run rate of 2.5 per over. But they laboured hard against the opening and first change attacks. At tea, they were 50 for 2, Barry Dudleston and Roger Tolchard having gone cheaply, and Leicestershire were well below the required striking rate. Of course they still had plenty of wickets in hand and Yorkshire had yet to introduce John Woodford, the weakest of their five bowlers, but it was quite easy to foresee a collapse as Leicestershire became forced to step up the tempo.

The departure of Brian Davison three overs into the final session caused another brief heart flutter, but a stand of 26 between Mick Norman and Balderstone was the first significant partnership of the innings and finally put Leicestershire on the way. Norman had scored 38 when he fell to a Phil Sharpe slip catch off

Tony Nicholson

Woodford's bowling and Ray Illingworth could only score 5 before he was out.

But with 15 overs left and 40 runs needed, the die was cast. Chris Balderstone's confidence was mirrored by Paul Hayward and for the first time we saw two batsmen prepared to commit themselves to the front foot and go for their shots. The winning runs scored by Hayward were a signal for thousands of delighted Leicestershire fans to storm the pitch.

BENSON AND HEDGES CUP FINAL 1972

Played at Lord's, 22 July
Toss: Yorkshire
Result: Leicestershire won by five wickets
Gold Award: Chris Balderstone
Adjudicator: Peter May

YORKSHIRE

			Fall of Wickets	
P.J. Sharpe	c Tolchard b Higgs	14	1st	17
R.G. Lumb	b McKenzie	7	2nd	21
B. Leadbeater	run out	32	3rd	60
J.H. Hampshire	lbw b McKenzie	14	4th	65
R.A. Hutton	c Spencer b Steele	8	5th	77
J.D. Woodford	c Spencer b Illingworth	1	6th	83
C. Johnson	b Higgs	20	7th	113
C.M. Old	lbw b Illingworth	6	8th	122
D.L. Bairstow	c Tolchard b McKenzie	13	9th	124
H.P. Cooper	not out	7		
A. Nicholson	not out	4		
Extras (lb 9 nb 1)		10		
Total (55 overs)		**136 for 9**		

LEICESTERSHIRE

			Fall of Wickets	
B. Dudleston	c Bairstow b Nicholson	6	1st	16
M.E.J.C. Norman	c Sharpe b Woodford	38	2nd	24
R.W. Tolchard	c Bairstow b Cooper	3	3rd	58
B.F. Davison	b Cooper	17	4th	84
J.C. Balderstone	not out	41	5th	97
R. Illingworth	c Bairstow b Hutton	5		
P.R. Hayward	not out	21		
J.F. Steele	did not bat			
G.D. McKenzie	did not bat			
K. Higgs	did not bat			
C.T. Spencer	did not bat			
Extras (b 2 lb 2 w 4 nb 1)		9		
Total (46.5 overs)		**140 for 5**		

LEICESTERSHIRE	O	M	R	W		YORKSHIRE	O	M	R	W
McKenzie	11	2	22	3		Old	9.5	1	35	0
Higgs	11	1	33	2		Nicholson	9	2	17	1
Spencer	7	2	11	0		Hutton	11	1	24	1
Davison	11	2	22	0		Cooper	9	0	27	2
Illingworth	10	3	21	2		Woodford	8	1	28	1
Steele	5	1	17	1						

Umpires D.J. Constant and T.W. Spencer

1973
KENT v WORCESTERSHIRE

Not many readers will realise from Kent's 39-run win what a close game this Benson and Hedges Final really was. Before Basil D'Oliveira was out in the 47th over, the suspicion had gradually been growing that Worcestershire had it in them to pull a sensational victory out of the bag and it became momentarily rather more than a suspicion when D'Oliveira's last scoring stroke was a hooked six off Asif Iqbal. At that point, Worcestershire needed 58 to win from 8.3 overs, which in the context of D'Oliveira and Gifford's stand of 70 in 12 overs was distinctly on. But D'Oliveira was out next ball!

It was another of those incredible days when it was raining everywhere but Lord's. It sounded from the forecast that the Lord's luck had run out. Yet after a showery morning, when it twice rained almost hard enough for the players to come off, the day brightened.

Kent's opener Graham Johnson was first to go when he was run out by Jim Cumbes and with the score still on 23, skipper Mike Denness, who had won the toss and decided to bat, was caught at mid-on by Basil D'Oliveira at the same total off the bowling of Cumbes.

Kent had been pedestrian in starting, for the 23 runs came off 12 overs and by the time the 20th had been completed, their score was still only 34. Then Luckhurst and Asif Iqbal began to take control of the bowling and with Luckhurst hammering a mighty six off D'Oliveira, he and Asif showed they meant business. Singles were taken at every opportunity but in the fifth over after lunch, Luckhurst's innings ended when he had made 79. Trying to take a second run after hitting Ivan Johnson through the covers, Jim Yardley's throw was perfectly placed for wicket-keeper Rodney Cass to run him out. He had hit three fours and a six and with Asif put on 115 runs in 28 overs.

The Pakistani Test star should have been run out when he had scored 48 but Worcestershire skipper Norman Gifford threw the ball in much too high for Cass to take. Ivan Johnson dropped a difficult chance offered close to the wicket by Asif

Brian Luckhurst

Basil D'Oliveira

and Ealham was nearly run out following a smart piece of fielding by Cumbes. Asif completed his half-century in 99 minutes but incredibly for him, there had been only one boundary. He was eventually out for 59 bowled by Gifford, after Ealham had been caught in the gully by Ron Headley off Johnson.

John Shepherd and Colin Cowdrey scored freely before Shepherd skied a Brian Brain delivery to Gifford. Alan Knott was the last Kent man to fall, run out off the last ball when Kent were 225 for 7.

Worcestershire's innings revolved round Norman Gifford's use of his left-handers, whom in two cases, Cass and his own, he sent in out of order expressly to get after Underwood, who with Woolmer was clearly the main obstacle to an asking-rate of four runs per over.

Headley and Turner started off at a cracking rate but then Kent's opening bowlers Graham and Asif began to tie them down. The West Indian was caught behind and then in the last over before tea, the New

Norman Gifford

Zealander was bowled by Woolmer. Ted Hemsley was run out for 23 following an on target throw-in by Alan Ealham, and Alan Ormrod provided Asif with his first victim when he took a fine caught and bowled chance. Cass lost his wicket when he lost patience with Underwood and tried the big hit, which was comfortably taken by the Kent skipper Mike Denness at mid-on.

Basil D'Oliveira then came in at No. 7 to join his skipper with 128 needed for victory from 20.2 overs. It was a bad oversight to hold back his best player to bat so far down the order and 'Dolly' – his striking was as superb as his improvisation – certainly rubbed it in by scoring 47 from 48 balls, showing how the match might have been won.

The ground rose to him, and later on to Gifford, whose unsettling of Shepherd, whom he charged, had been a big factor in Worcestershire's scoring 96 in the 17 overs he was batting. Had D'Oliveira and Gifford stayed together, the result could have gone the other way, for Kent were certainly getting the jitters. After they had gone, the Worcestershire tail failed to give even a flutter of hope and the last three wickets fell for only five runs!

In the end, Worcestershire lost by 39 runs, almost the difference between the highest partnerships between the respective counties.

GOLD AWARD WINNER 1973
ASIF IQBAL

Asif Iqbal was just 17 when he played for Hyderabad in the Ranji Trophy, and when Pakistan toured India in 1961 he represented the South Zone against them. Around this time, most of his family, who were Muslims, had emigrated to Pakistan, and Asif later joined them.

In 1963, the Pakistan Eaglets, comprising promising youngsters and a fair number of Test players, left for a short tour of England. His performances on this tour led to him winning the first of 58 Test caps, when he scored 41 batting at No. 10 in the match against Australia at Karachi. At the beginning of 1967 he was made captain to face an MCC Under 25 team.

The MCC manager was Les Ames and he at once recognised Asif's leadership qualities. In their second encounter, Asif hit his maiden first-class hundred – an innings that guaranteed him the trip to England.

During the Oval test, Asif hit 146 in three hours, the highest score by a No. 9 in a Test match. In his first appearance against Kent, Colin Cowdrey sounded him out about joining the hop county. Asif joined Kent in 1968, bringing with him an uninhibited brand of cricket.

Asif was a batsman of quality, a bowler who could cut or swing the ball and a fielder with superb reflexes. In 1970, he was at the peak of his powers, scoring 1,379 runs at 39.40; the following summer he hit 91 in an innings that nearly brought Kent victory against Lancashire in the Gillette Cup Final. On six occasions Asif scored a thousand or more runs for Kent in the County Championship, and he captained the side in 1977 and 1981–82 with great inspiration.

At Test level, he hit three centuries in four different series during 1976–77. Against New Zealand he scored 166, helping Javed Miandad set a fifth wicket record of 281. In Australia he averaged 78.25, scoring 313 runs including centuries at Adelaide (152 not out) and Sydney (120), following it with 135 against the West Indies at Kingston, Jamaica.

It was Asif who used the Packer Affair in a positive way to get better money for all Pakistan's cricketers. He was a constant and thrilling match-winner for both Kent and Pakistan and he scored 13,231 runs for the hop county at 37.06.

BENSON AND HEDGES CUP FINAL 1973

Played at Lord's, 21 July
Toss: Kent
Result: Kent won by 39 runs
Gold Award: Asif Iqbal
Adjudicator: Sir Len Hutton

KENT

			Fall of Wickets	
B.W. Luckhurst	run out	79	1st	23
G.W. Johnson	run out	9	2nd	23
M.H. Denness	c D'Oliveira b Cumbes	0	3rd	139
Asif Iqbal	b Gifford	59	4th	165
A.G.E. Ealham	c Headley b Johnson	15	5th	172
J.N. Shepherd	c Gifford b Brain	12	6th	198
M.C. Cowdrey	not out	29	7th	225
A.P.E. Knott	run out	12		
R.A. Woolmer	did not bat			
D.L. Underwood	did not bat			
J.N. Graham	did not bat			
Extras (b 4 lb 5 nb 1)		10		
Total (55 overs)		**225 for 7**		

WORCESTERSHIRE

			Fall of Wickets	
R.G.A. Headley	c Knott b Graham	13	1st	26
G.M. Turner	b Woolmer	25	2nd	57
E.J.O. Hemsley	run out	23	3rd	69
G.R. Cass	c Denness b Underwood	19	4th	85
J.A. Ormrod	c and b Asif	12	5th	98
N. Gifford	b Asif	33	6th	168
B.L. D'Oliveira	c Underwood b Asif	47	7th	181
T.J. Yardley	not out	3	8th	184
I.N. Johnson	b Shepherd	2	9th	185
B.M. Brain	b Asif	0	10th	186
J. Cumbes	run out	1		
Extras (lb 8)		8		
Total (51.4 overs)		**186 all out**		

WORCESTERSHIRE

	O	M	R	W
Brain	11	2	26	1
Cumbes	11	1	37	1
Gifford	11	2	46	1
D'Oliveira	11	2	45	0
Hemsley	2	0	17	0
Johnson	9	0	44	1

KENT

	O	M	R	W
Graham	9	0	38	1
Asif Iqbal	11	1	43	4
Shepherd	11	0	41	1
Woolmer	11	0	36	1
Underwood	9.4	1	20	1

Umpires C.S. Elliott and A.E.G. Rhodes

1974
SURREY v LEICESTERSHIRE

For virtually all of this match, it seemed that Surrey, desperately eager for so long to win a limited-overs competition, would have to be satisfied with the bouquets that runners-up receive! Their total of 170 seemed much too slight and after the first ball dismissal of Dudleston, Steele and Norman had taken Leicestershire to 46 for 1. Then 4 wickets fell for just 19 runs – indeed 3 for 4 – and it was suddenly quite apparent that John Edrich's tight field settings and his timely switching of his four main seam bowlers would ensure his side a narrow victory.

Surrey had begun grimly, Skinner failing to trouble the scorers as he was leg-before to Higgs. New Zealand Test player Geoff Howarth looked confident, scoring 22 runs in quick-time before edging Peter Booth to wicket-keeper Tolchard. Booth and McKenzie made the occasional ball fly, but Younis Ahmed, who had joined Edrich at the crease, stroked freely and strongly. Though he scored just 18 runs in the first 24 overs, Edrich's stubborn resistance helped take Surrey to 99 before they lost their third wicket – Younis Ahmed, the highest scorer of the match with 43, chipping Illingworth to Barry Dudleston.

While Edrich remained at the crease, Surrey seemed to have the upper hand, but when he was out for a painstaking 40, offering a low return catch to slow left-armer John Steele in the 36th over, Surrey's worst hour approached. Roope was out of touch and lost his off-stump to McKenzie, while Storey, who was leg-before to Illingworth, was handicapped by an Achilles tendon injury which had necessitated painkilling injections.

In the 44th over, Peter Booth at mid-off dropped Robin Jackman when he had scored six. He went on to make a further 30 runs before Ken Higgs then made sure that the later batsmen did not get away with a challenging target. The former Lancashire paceman performed the hat-trick to dismiss Alan Butcher, Pat Pocock and Arnold Long – it is the only hat-trick ever taken in a Benson and Hedges Cup Final. He finished with 4 for 10 in his seven overs and Surrey were all out for 170 in the last over. But, looking back, Leicestershire could have done with it half-an-hour earlier!

Geoff Arnold made sure Leicestershire had the worst possible start when Barry Dudleston was adjudged leg-before off the first ball of their innings. Steele and Norman steadied the ship with a partnership of 46 before the latter fell to Graham Roope. This was the start of the

Geoff Arnold

Robin Jackman

Leicestershire collapse for, without any addition to the score, Steele found himself at the same end as Davison and was run out. With the score on 50, Tolchard was also lbw to Roope – an interesting decision, which appeared – admittedly to those side-on – as if it may well have been a case of the umpire refusing to accept that the forward stroke offered was genuine. It was one of four instances during the day when Bill Alley donned his black hat in response to lbw shouts.

Davison's wicket, probably the most important, went somewhat unexpectedly when he slashed a ball from Arnold breastbone-high to Howarth at cover. That was 65 for 5. Seven runs later, Pat Pocock took over from Butcher, and Surrey achieved their objective in a smoothly professional manner.

Though Balderstone and Illingworth advanced the score to 113, the Leicestershire captain was batting on only one and a half legs! Pocock bowled Balderstone, Leicestershire's top scorer, for 32 before forcing McVicker to offer the simplest of catches to Edrich. McKenzie was smartly stumped down the leg-side by Arnold Long next ball before Jackman had Booth caught at cover by Arnold. The Surrey paceman bowled Illingworth in the penultimate over with 28 runs still needed, to finish with 3 for 20 while Pocock's off-breaks took 3 for 26.

Despite their defeat, Leicestershire's supporters were still in good voice, but now it was at the expense of Freddie Brown, who could barely make himself heard at the presentation. The Gold Award went to Surrey skipper John Edrich for his fortifying innings and leadership in the field and the Benson and Hedges Cup was handed to a team of cricketers who could at last answer back when they were reminded of the glorious 1950s.

GOLD AWARD WINNER 1974
JOHN EDRICH

A cousin of the former Middlesex and England batsman Bill Edrich, John opted to join Surrey and in 1959, his first full season, he made 1,799 runs, including a century in each innings of his second Championship match against Nottinghamshire at Trent Bridge.

A left-handed opening batsman who could bat at No. 3 with equal success, Edrich tended to restrict himself to a few highly profitable strokes until he was thoroughly established. He missed little on or outside his legs and off either back or front foot he scored many runs square of cover-point. Small and sturdily built, he worked out a method of batting that was safer than it often looked and that, with his great resolution, served him and his side well.

Edrich played his first Test against the West Indies in 1963 – failed and was dropped. The following summer he came back and scored a century against Australia but after several failures was dropped again. He did not find it easy to get back into the England side but in 1965 in the third Test against New Zealand, he came back with the highest score ever made by an Englishman at Headingley: 310 not out, made in almost nine hours!

Yet even then he found himself in and out of the side until 1968 against Australia when he was ensconced. At Test level, he went on to score 5,138 runs at 43.54 with 12 centuries.

Edrich captained Surrey for five seasons without any great success but his men would have followed him almost through the kind of fire that he accepted as normal for himself.

In 1977 he was made an MBE and Surrey, who had truly appreciated him, gave him two Testimonials. Only two left-handers, Philip Mead and Frank Woolley, scored more centuries than John Edrich, who in 1981 became a selector. But after a single year he gave up the office as it did not keep him busy enough. He was always a busy, brave, cheerful man.

BENSON AND HEDGES CUP FINAL 1974

Played at Lord's, 20 July
Toss: Surrey
Result: Surrey won by 27 runs
Gold Award: John Edrich
Adjudicator: Freddie Brown

SURREY

				Fall of Wickets	
J.H. Edrich	c and b Steele	40		1st	4
L.E. Skinner	lbw b Higgs	0		2nd	36
G.P. Howarth	c Tolchard b Booth	22		3rd	99
Younis Ahmed	c Dudleston b Booth	43		4th	111
G.R.J. Roope	b McKenzie	13		5th	118
S.J. Storey	lbw b Illingworth	2		6th	137
R.D. Jackman	c Tolchard b McKenzie	36		7th	168
A.R. Butcher	c Tolchard b Higgs	7		8th	168
P.I. Pocock	b Higgs	0		9th	168
A. Long	c Tolchard b Higgs	0		10th	170
G.G. Arnold	not out	0			
Extras (lb 5 nb 2)		7			
Total (54.1 overs)		**170 all out**			

LEICESTERSHIRE

				Fall of Wickets	
B. Dudleston	lbw b Arnold	0		1st	0
J.F. Steele	run out	18		2nd	46
M.E.J.C. Norman	lbw b Roope	24		3rd	46
B.F. Davison	c Howarth b Arnold	13		4th	50
R.W. Tolchard	lbw b Roope	0		5th	65
J.C. Balderstone	b Pocock	32		6th	113
R. Illingworth	b Arnold	23		7th	129
N.M. McVicker	c Edrich b Pocock	10		8th	129
G.D. McKenzie	st Long b Pocock	0		9th	131
P. Booth	c Arnold b Jackman	5		10th	143
K. Higgs	not out	8			
Extras (b 1 lb 5 nb 4)		10			
Total (54 overs)		**143 all out**			

LEICESTERSHIRE	O	M	R	W	SURREY	O	M	R	W
McKenzie	10.1	0	31	2	Arnold	10	4	20	3
Higgs	7	2	10	4	Jackman	11	1	34	1
Booth	8	1	30	1	Roope	11	2	30	2
McVicker	8	1	25	0	Butcher	11	1	23	0
Illingworth	11	0	36	2	Pocock	11	1	26	3
Steele	10	0	31	1					

Umpires W.E. Alley and H.D. Bird

1975

MIDDLESEX v LEICESTERSHIRE

Leicestershire, who were in their third Benson and Hedges Cup Final in four years, not only beat some good teams to reach Lord's but beat them with fair comfort. Middlesex on the other hand had got there by the proverbial skin of their teeth. There were defeats by Essex and Kent and victories over Sussex and Minor Counties (South) to send them through to the quarter-finals. Then came an efficient victory over Yorkshire and a pulsating last-ball victory over Warwickshire at Edgbaston. But it was not Middlesex's day, even though Mike Brearley won the toss and did the old-fashioned thing by batting.

Mike Brearley

The Middlesex innings never picked up at all – although it couldn't have been helped by a 40-minute hold up for rain shortly after the start. Anyone who came just too late for the first over missed the best stroke of the match – Phil Edmonds hooking McKenzie into the Mound Stand for six. It was anyone's guess whether the break would affect Middlesex more than the wet ball would Leicestershire's seamers.

We were soon to know and Norman McVicker ripped in with a 3 for 3 burst in four overs. His first ball was driven uppishly into the covers by Edmonds where Illingworth made ground to take the catch two-handed. Radley, who had survived two lbw shouts by McKenzie, was beautifully caught low down by Higgs at slip as he attempted to cut. Middlesex had barely recovered from that blow when, at 43, McVicker struck again. Brearley drove him hard and low for what seemed certain to be four but Davison flung himself to his right and picked up a breath-taking catch inches from the ground. McVicker then clinched his second

Phil Edmonds

'Man of the Match' award in a week by getting Norman Featherstone caught behind and Middlesex's innings lay virtually in ruins at 87 for 4 and only 19 overs left.

Larry Gomes and Barlow played on to Higgs and Illingworth respectively and Smith had seen the departure of the last two recognised batsmen in Murray and Titmus by the 50th over with just 119 on the board. Murray decided to hit out and was beautifully taken by Graham Cross, while Titmus's dismissal was, to all but the Middlesex fans, hilarious. He and Smith got into such a tangle as to whether or not they should take a second run but the off-spinner was not amused when the ball arrived in Tolchard's gloves some time before he had regained his ground.

Mike Smith was finally out in the 51st over, well caught by Roger Tolchard. Smith hit only four boundaries and played and missed, edged, mis-hit, but did a magnificent job for his side. Only two other batsmen made it into double figures.

Mike Smith

Leicestershire, as they had done right through the competition, performed well in the field. Apart from the catching, the ground fielding was breathtaking and each of the seven bowlers used gave absolutely nothing away. Barring disaster, Middlesex's total of 146 seemed well within reach.

Barry Dudleston and John Steele had moved comfortably to 32 in 13 overs when Dudleston backed up much too far and was easily run out by Brearley's throw from mid-wicket. Balderstone and Steele, however, took the total on to 67 with overs and seemingly the Cup in the bag. Then things started to go wrong!

Steele dabbed Gomes away on the off-side and they went for a run but Radley at short cover threw down the stumps with Balderstone well out of his ground. Then Davison fell almost immediately without troubling the scorers. Middlesex gave nothing away and in the next 13 overs, the scoreboard advanced by only 27 runs.

It might have been an unkind exaggeration but Middlesex's best chance of winning was to keep Steele in! In the 39th over, Price, off a short run, beat his bat three times but twelve runs off Edmonds's next over got things moving again.

Titmus with a six-three leg field was a constant threat and had Steele top-edging to leg slip and Cross sweeping fatally but only a dramatic wicket-taking spell was going to deny Leicestershire.

Tolchard's impudent running was having its effect. Playing deliberately for overthrows, he twice pinched runs in that way. Illingworth, with that inbuilt sense of theatre was, however, the man who finished it all off, hitting Selvey for an all-run four and hooking his next ball to the square-leg fence.

There hasn't been much in cricket that Illy hasn't achieved, but no one's smile was broader when he collected the trophy – Leicestershire winning the Cup for the second time in three attempts in the competition's four years.

GOLD AWARD WINNER 1975
NORMAN McVICKER

Not many first-class cricketers graduate into the first-class game from the Minor Counties, and fewer still from Minor County cricket when they reach the age of 28. Though Norman McVicker had a trial for Lancashire as a youngster, they didn't think that he had the physique for a fast bowler and it came to nothing. McVicker was working for a tobacco company in Manchester when he had the offer to join a firm in Lincolnshire. He accepted and soon started to play for the county. That was in 1963, when he was also chosen to play for the Minor Counties against the Australians. One or two first-class counties became interested in him, and in 1969 he joined Warwickshire.

McVicker, who in his early days modelled himself on Lancashire and England paceman Brian Statham, spent five seasons at Edgbaston. In 1971 he performed the hat-trick against his former side Lincolnshire in a Gillette Cup match, while his best bowling for the county came in his first season when he took 7 for 29 against Northamptonshire at Edgbaston. At the end of the 1973 season, McVicker, who had taken 306 wickets for Warwickshire at a cost of 26.06 runs apiece, left to play for Leicestershire. In his first season with the county, Leicestershire won the John Player Sunday League and reached the Benson and Hedges Cup Final.

The right-arm, fast-medium bowler had an outstanding summer in 1975. His 482 runs and 46 wickets at a cost of 25.82 runs apiece helped Leicestershire to their first ever County Championship. Surprisingly for McVicker, who took 38 wickets in the Benson and Hedges Cup at a cost of 20.23, while conceding just 3.16 runs per over, this was his only Gold Award!

After three seasons at Grace Road, the affable McVicker, who was then 35, decided to leave the first-class game, having taken 413 wickets for his two counties at a cost of 25.47 runs each.

BENSON AND HEDGES CUP FINAL 1975

Played at Lord's, 19 July
Toss: Middlesex
Result: Leicestershire won by five wickets
Gold Award: Norman McVicker
Adjudicator: Ted Dexter

MIDDLESEX

			Fall of Wickets	
M.J. Smith	c Tolchard b Booth	83	1st	26
P.H. Edmonds	c Illingworth b McVicker	11	2nd	37
C.T. Radley	c Higgs b McVicker	7	3rd	43
J.M. Brearley	c Davison b McVicker	2	4th	87
N.G. Featherstone	c Tolchard b McVicker	11	5th	99
H.A. Gomes	b Higgs	3	6th	110
G.D. Barlow	b Illingworth	7	7th	117
J.T. Murray	c Cross b Steele	1	8th	119
F.J. Titmus	run out	0	9th	141
M.W.W. Selvey	c Tolchard b Booth	6	10th	146
J.S.E. Price	not out	2		
Extras (lb 10 nb 3)		13		
Total (52.4 overs)		**146 all out**		

LEICESTERSHIRE

			Fall of Wickets	
B. Dudleston	run out	17	1st	32
J.F. Steele	c Selvey b Titmus	49	2nd	67
J.C. Balderstone	run out	12	3rd	67
B.F. Davison	c Murray b Gomes	0	4th	118
R.W. Tolchard	not out	47	5th	121
G.F. Cross	lbw b Titmus	0		
R. Illingworth	not out	13		
N.M. McVicker	did not bat			
P. Booth	did not bat			
G. McKenzie	did not bat			
K. Higgs	did not bat			
Extras (b 3 lb 9)		12		
Total (51.2 overs)		**150 for 5**		

MIDDLESEX	O	M	R	W
McKenzie	7	2	20	0
Higgs	10	3	18	1
McVicker	11	3	20	4
Booth	8.4	1	25	2
Cross	2	0	9	0
Illingworth	9	1	31	1
Steele	5	0	10	1

LEICESTERSHIRE	O	M	R	W
Price	9	3	26	0
Selvey	9.2	2	33	0
Titmus	11	2	30	2
Gomes	11	4	22	1
Edmonds	11	2	27	0

Umpires W.L. Budd and A.E. Fagg

1976
KENT v WORCESTERSHIRE

The fifth Benson and Hedges Cup Final went to Kent who beat Worcestershire by 43 runs – an almost identical result to that produced by the same teams in the 1973 Final. Considering the disarray Worcestershire found themselves in during the winter months, it was a most pleasant surprise to find them at Lord's. When they won the toss and gave Kent's batsmen presumably the worst of the day's atmospheric conditions, there was a slight shift in the betting further towards Norman Gifford and his men.

Worcestershire's bowling was very ordinary and certainly they could not afford to lose Basil D'Oliveira, who went off with hamstring trouble, after sending down four overs for 21 runs. Quite apart from the loss of his bowling, Worcestershire needed his batting.

After 15 overs, however, when Johnson and Bob Woolmer, though stroking the ball handsomely, had made only 44, Worcestershire, if not strong favourites, had the match seemingly under control. In the 25th over, Graham Johnson was missed by Turner at square-leg off Pridgeon, and in the 29th over, Woolmer, having hit Gifford sweetly, once among the seats in front of the pavilion, was well caught at wide long-on by John Inchmore. Mike Denness, who had been troubled by a knee injury before the match, came in. By the 40th over, when he was out, caught behind off the bowling of Inchmore, Kent were only 155.

Worcestershire, restricting Kent at this stage to around four an over, gained another success when Graham Johnson's innings ended when he had scored 78. Boyns, called on to replace the injured D'Oliveira, bowled him as the Kent opener danced down the wicket to attempt a big hit.

Asif Iqbal

A lightning return throw by Glen Turner would have run out Ealham had Boyns taken the ball cleanly but the Shropshire-born youngster quickly earned revenge. Ealham tried to lift him over mid-off but put the ball into Ormrod's hands. Boyns bowled his 11 overs respectably

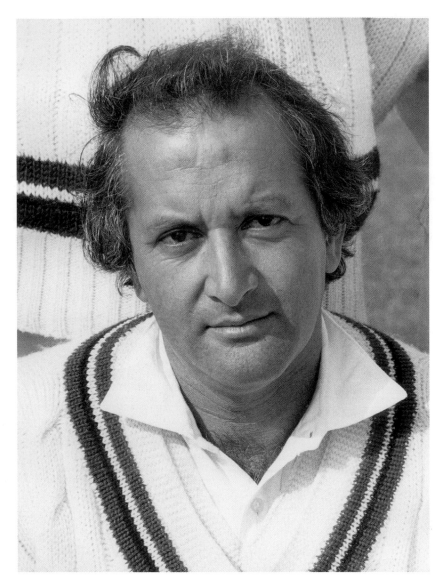

Basil D'Oliveira

well, Gifford as ever was tight and the field-placing solid. Asif gave up trying to pierce it towards the end and settled for a series of twos, when perhaps only singles would have been on offer to average runners-between-wickets. His usual improvisations in an innings of 48 not out took the Kent score to 236 for 7, the highest total yet in a Benson and Hedges Final.

Worcestershire must have felt capable of overtaking it. D'Oliveira may well have been crippled but Glenn Turner and Alan Ormrod were one of the best opening pairs in the country and Imran Khan was a major force.

The Worcestershire openers made a fair start, until the first bowling change brought on West Indian all-rounder John Shepherd. Turner had made just 14 when he was caught behind off Shepherd, and Phil Neale, coming in ahead of Imran, soon fell to the same bowler. The rate lagged against Kent's as the overs went by and when Ormrod fell to Derek Underwood and Imran was caught high up at cover off a firm hit, it really all depended on whether the hobbling Basil D'Oliveira could get the necessary runs in boundaries!

D'Oliveira arrived at the crease with Turner as his runner and the Worcestershire score on 126 for 5. Swinging from a static position, he pounded the cover field and the forward leg field, staggering away from the wicket after each blow and watching Turner scuttle up and down for his runs, first with Hemsley and later with the eager Boyns. Soon after wicket-keeper Wilcock joined him, D'Oliveira, having hit five fours and a six, was bowled off the inside edge by Jarvis for a quite superb half-century and the match was decided. He limped off to a standing ovation, while Kevin Jarvis, who was at the time being spoken of as one of the sharpest young fast bowlers around, destroyed Worcestershire's tail, as a good fast bowler should and they succumbed to 193 all out.

For his 78 and four catches, Graham Johnson received the Gold Award from Sir Gary Sobers; in this instance, perhaps it could have gone to someone on the losing side who made a one-sided game into a contest!

GOLD AWARD WINNER 1976
GRAHAM JOHNSON

When Graham Johnson joined the Kent staff, it was primarily as an off-spin bowler but he developed into a batsman who also bowled. Though he made his Kent debut in 1965, his first team chances were rather limited due to the fact that Underwood and the Kent seamers were bowling well. By 1970 he was an established member of the Kent side and played a significant part in their Championship success that summer, scoring 927 runs.

When Underwood was away on Test duty, Johnson had an opportunity to bowl. Though he rarely ran through a side, he performed with great consistency, adding variety to an all-seam attack. He also had the knack of picking up wickets at crucial times, and as the 1970s wore on he became an essential part of the Kent bowling line-up. In 1973, Johnson passed 1,000 runs in a season for the first time, scoring 1,362 runs at 33.42. He achieved this feat for three successive seasons, culminating with his 1,366 runs in 1975, the most runs scored by a Kent player that summer.

A cartilage operation and a series of niggling injuries restricted Johnson's appearances over the next couple of seasons. When he did return to action, he found himself opening the innings at one-day level but batting at No. 7 in the Championship, and many Kent followers thought he had found his real niche in the game.

When Mike Denness departed at the end of the 1976 season, Johnson was overlooked for the captaincy. He went on to play for Kent under various captains, his adaptability in changing circumstances serving him well.

In his twenty years with Kent, Johnson scored 12,549 runs and took 555 wickets – but he was one of many good county cricketers whose statistics do not do justice to their many talents. He sacrificed his personal aims and ambitions to ensure Kent's success, always remaining an integral part of the county side.

BENSON AND HEDGES CUP FINAL 1976

Played at Lord's, 17 July
Toss: Worcestershire
Result: Kent won by 43 runs
Gold Award: Graham Johnson
Adjudicator: Sir Garfield Sobers

KENT

Batsman	Dismissal	Runs		Fall of Wickets	
G.W. Johnson	b Boyns	78	1st	110	
R.A. Woolmer	c Inchmore b Gifford	61	2nd	155	
M.H. Denness	c Wilcock b Inchmore	15	3rd	171	
Asif Iqbal	not out	48	4th	194	
A.G.E. Ealham	c Ormrod b Boyns	11	5th	215	
J.N. Shepherd	c Boyns b Gifford	8	6th	220	
A.P.E. Knott	b Imran Khan	1	7th	236	
C.J.C. Rowe	run out	0			
R.W. Hills	did not bat				
D.L. Underwood	did not bat				
K.B.S. Jarvis	did not bat				
Extras (b 2 lb 10 nb 2)		14			
Total (55 overs)		**236 for 7**			

WORCESTERSHIRE

Batsman	Dismissal	Runs		Fall of Wickets	
J.A. Ormrod	c Johnson b Underwood	37	1st	40	
G.M. Turner	c Knott b Shepherd	14	2nd	52	
P.A. Neale	c Johnson b Shepherd	5	3rd	70	
Imran Khan	c Johnson b Underwood	12	4th	90	
E.J.O. Hemsley	c Johnson b Underwood	15	5th	126	
B.L. D'Oliveira	b Jarvis	50	6th	161	
C.N. Boyns	c Knott b Jarvis	15	7th	166	
H.G. Wilcock	not out	19	8th	172	
N. Gifford	c Knott b Jarvis	0	9th	175	
J.D. Inchmore	c Underwood b Asif Iqbal	2	10th	193	
A.P. Pridgeon	b Jarvis	8			
Extras (b 1 lb 12 w 1 nb 2)		16			
Total (52.4 overs)		**193 all out**			

WORCESTERSHIRE

	O	M	R	W
Imran Khan	9	1	26	1
Inchmore	11	0	57	1
Pridgeon	9	1	35	0
D'Oliveira	4	1	21	0
Gifford	11	3	38	2
Boyns	11	0	45	2

KENT

	O	M	R	W
Jarvis	10.4	2	34	4
Asif Iqbal	9	0	35	1
Shepherd	7	0	17	2
Woolmer	11	3	27	0
Underwood	9	2	31	3
Hills	6	0	33	0

Umpires D.J. Constant and T.W. Spencer

1977

GLOUCESTERSHIRE v KENT

It was not Gloucestershire's victory in the Benson and Hedges Cup Final so much as the ease and the size of it that were surprising. Kent went into the game with a slightly odd-looking side, preferring the inexperienced Grahame Clinton as an opening batsman to both Graham Johnson and Chris Cowdrey. In fact, Cowdrey had made a match-winning 114 in Kent's quarter-final defeat of Sussex and it was probably his omission that prevented them making a challenge to Gloucestershire's well-made but by no means unassailable 237 for 6.

There was no doubt that Kent had greater depth in both batting and bowling but on the day, Gloucestershire were stronger where it mattered – at the top of the order. Andy Stovold and Test players Sadiq Mohammed, Zaheer Abbas and Mike Procter, the first four in their batting order, and Procter and Brian Brain, their opening bowlers, outplayed their opposite numbers easily and the 64-run winning margin was no more than the Gloucestershire side's play deserved.

Gloucestershire made the running from the start with Stovold and Sadiq Mohammed plundering 19 runs from the first two overs from Kevin Jarvis and West Indian Bernard Julien to immediately seize the initiative. The pair had taken the score to 79 when Sadiq clipped the ball into the hands of Richard Hills off the bowling of Bob Woolmer. The Pakistani opener, who made 24, had been limited to a supporting role as Stovold hit ten fours in a no-nonsense type of innings that shook Kent by its early briskness. Any fears that Sadiq's dismissal would lead to another collapse – Gloucestershire had gone from 121 for 1 to 180 all out in the semi-final win over Hampshire – were quickly dispelled as the magical Zaheer Abbas took centre-stage. He too had to play second fiddle to Andy Stovold, who after hitting ten fours, eventually went for an entertaining 71 after hitting Shepherd to Underwood on the leg-side.

He had flagged a little against Derek Underwood but there is no more frustrating form of bowling than accurate left-arm round the wicket, pitching leg stump and outside to a six-man leg field. Underwood did this to perfection; though his 11 overs did not bring a wicket, they cost only 32 runs. Perhaps the only consolation from the supporters' viewpoint was the scope it gave Alan Knott for a wonderful display of wicket-keeping.

Stovold's departure left the way clear for Zaheer to dominate as only he could, sliding the ball through the offside and accelerating the scoring rate as the overs started to run out. Procter, executing two or three difficult pick-ups against Underwood, went for a typically hard-hit 25 while Zaheer followed soon after to leave the score at 204 for 4. Though Shepherd and Graveney fell cheaply to Jarvis and Julien respectively there was still time for Jim Foat to smash an unbeaten 21, including boundaries off the final two balls bowled by Kevin Jarvis.

Kent required 238 to win at a little more than four an over and normally would have expected to get there. But it certainly looked a tall order as the new ball pairing of Brain and Procter wrecked their hopes. Brain bowled Grahame Clinton for a duck and Procter had Charles Rowe caught behind by Stovold, also without troubling the scorers. Kent were like rabbits caught in the headlights as Brain opened up with four straight maidens and Procter

Alan Knott

looked like taking a wicket with every ball he bowled. Martin Vernon added the crucial wickets of Asif Iqbal and Alan Ealham cheaply, the latter to a leaping catch by Stovold that many a taller wicket-keeper would have been pleased to get a touch to, and when David Graveney bowled Bernard Julien, Kent were 65 for 5.

Bob Woolmer, who opened the Kent innings and watched the mayhem from the other end, was joined by John Shepherd and they threatened to turn the tide until Woolmer, with a lazy flick, knocked an easy catch to the man at deep mid-wicket. Alan Knott had already struck a defiant six but he was next out, caught on the square-leg boundary by Zaheer after trying to repeat the shot.

Julian Shackleton's dismissal of Richard Hills just about wrapped it up before Brain came back to mop up, bowling deadly Derek Underwood and then having last man John Shepherd caught by Procter for a brave and battling 55.

Only four Kent men reached double figures, and Gloucestershire eventually won with 45 balls to spare, sparking incredible scenes among their massed ranks of supporters.

hn Shepherd

GOLD AWARD WINNER 1977
ANDY STOVOLD

Andy Stovold made his Gloucestershire debut in 1973, a year after touring the West Indies with the England Young Cricketers side. His debut came during the Cheltenham Festival week when he was selected as a batsman but ended up keeping wicket because of an injury to Roy Swetman. From that very moment, it appeared that neither Gloucestershire nor Andy Stovold was quite sure whether he should become a batsman or a wicket-keeper!

During these early years he was keeping wicket and opening the batting and with the advent of one-day cricket he was to gain instant recognition in this field. Also during the close seasons of 1974 to 1976, Stovold tried to gain further experience by playing for the Orange Free State in South Africa in the Currie Cup competition. Awarded his county cap in 1976, he came close to being selected for the MCC winter tour with 63 victims and a batting average of 33.92. His batting went from strength to strength, Stovold making an exhilarating 196 against Nottinghamshire at Trent Bridge in 1977.

Following the emergence of Jack Russell, he gave up his wicket-keeping duties to concentrate solely on his batting. In 1982 he hit 1,338 runs with a career best knock of 212 against Northamptonshire, while in the following summer he scored his best aggregate total of 1,671 runs

Inclined to play off the back foot, it was the square-cut that brought him a high proportion of his 17,460 runs and this coupled with his 312 victims (268 caught and 44 stumped) provides testimony to the fact that in the 1970s there was a time when it was believed he would play for England – at least in the one-day game.

Now Director of Coaching, his spirit characterised Gloucestershire cricket and made them a side enjoyable to watch and for other counties to play against.

BENSON AND HEDGES CUP FINAL
Played at Lord's, 16 July
Toss: Gloucestershire
Result: Gloucestershire won by 64 runs
Gold Award: Andy Stovold
Adjudicator: Fred Trueman

GLOUCESTERSHIRE

Sadiq Mohammed	c Hills b Woolmer	24
A.W. Stovold	c Underwood b Shepherd	71
Zaheer Abbas	c Underwood b Jarvis	70
M.J. Procter	c Knott b Julien	25
J.C. Foat	not out	21
D.R. Shepherd	b Jarvis	9
D.A. Graveney	c Underwood b Julien	1
M.J. Vernon	not out	3
M.D. Partridge	did not bat	
J.H. Shackleton	did not bat	
B.M. Brain	did not bat	
Extras (lb 7 w 2 nb 4)		13
Total (55 overs)		**237 for 6**

Fall of Wickets
1st	79
2nd	144
3rd	191
4th	204
5th	220
6th	223

KENT

R.A. Woolmer	c Shackleton b Graveney	64
G.S. Clinton	b Brain	0
C.J.C. Rowe	c Stovold b Procter	0
Asif Iqbal	c Stovold b Vernon	5
A.G.E. Ealham	c Stovold b Vernon	11
B.D. Julien	b Graveney	1
J.N. Shepherd	c Procter b Brain	55
A.P.E. Knott	c Zaheer Abbas b Partridge	14
R.W. Hills	c Procter b Shackleton	6
D.L. Underwood	b Brain	8
K.B.S. Jarvis	not out	0
Extras (lb 7 nb 2)		9
Total (47.3 overs)		**173 all out**

Fall of Wickets
1st	4
2nd	5
3rd	24
4th	64
5th	65
6th	100
7th	122
8th	150
9th	166
10th	173

KENT
	O	M	R	W
Jarvis	11	2	52	2
Julien	11	0	51	2
Shepherd	11	0	47	1
Woolmer	11	0	42	1
Underwood	11	1	32	0

GLOUCESTERSHIRE
	O	M	R	W
Procter	7	1	15	1
Brain	7.3	5	9	3
Vernon	11	1	52	2
Shackleton	10	0	40	1
Graveney	9	2	26	2
Partridge	3	0	22	1

Umpires H.D. Bird and W.L. Budd

1978

DERBYSHIRE v KENT

Kent returned to Lord's for their third final in a row, hoping to make up for the disappointment of losing to Gloucestershire the previous year. Captained by Alan Ealham, their third captain in three years, Kent were the clear favourites against a Derbyshire side led by South African all-rounder Eddie Barlow.

This was Derbyshire's first visit to Lord's as Benson and Hedges Cup finalists; in fact, it was the first year that the county had survived the zonal rounds! But their dreams of glory disintegrated as Kent won by six wickets with more than 13 overs to spare – in effect, they strolled it!

Kent needed only 148 to win and, expert as Derbyshire had been at defending low totals, there was no real pressure on the batsmen. It needed only one of them to play a substantial innings and the game was won.

Bob Woolmer did just that, scoring 79, and this, added to his bowling, earned him the Gold Award. This was a bit of a test for the adjudicator, Alec Bedser, who was at the time chairman of the selectors, since Woolmer was a member of Kerry Packer's World Series, the rival organisation which had disrupted the international scene.

Alan Ealham

Barlow had won the toss and decided to bat under the clouds. When Derbyshire opener Alan Hill emerged from the pavilion, he became the first batsman to wear a helmet in a Benson and Hedges Final.

Tony Borrington, who had had the plaster removed from his fractured wrist less than 48 hours earlier, was never in touch and fell to the first of Paul Downton's three catches. The gamble of thrusting Borrington back in had failed and when Hill was quite brilliantly caught by the diving Tavare at second slip and Barlow yorked by Derek Underwood, Derbyshire were in trouble at 33 for 3.

Underwood and Woolmer were in harness by then, and completely throttling the batsmen. Miller and Kirsten tried little more ambitious than survival but as the overs ticked away, it became more and more

Derek Underwood

Mike Hendrick

obvious that these two had to see it through and then open out. For a time, Kirsten played beautifully, but when he had made 41, he mistimed a hook shot off Asif and was comfortably held at long-leg by John Shepherd.

All depended on Geoff Miller but when he lost his off-stump to Shepherd, the end was near. Redeemed only by a gritty little tenth wicket stand between Wincer and Hendrick, the last six Derbyshire wickets fell for the addition of just 26 runs!

Derbyshire's bowlers had it all to do, but the odds were stacked against them because Kent had not the slightest need to take risks. Only twice did Derbyshire's hopes flicker, when Phil Russell took a couple of quick wickets and when Mike Hendrick returned to bowl an absolutely magnificent second spell.

Kent had reached 32 when Russell broke through in his second over, having Graham Johnson well taken at slip by Barlow. In his next over, Russell bowled Chris Tavare and completed his spell with a third wicket when Asif Iqbal, cutting, was caught by wicket-keeper Bob Taylor. When the pressure was on him, Phil Russell produced as good and as important a spell as he has ever bowled.

At tea, Kent were 50 for 3. If Derbyshire had been able to capture a quick wicket or two they would have been back in the contest, even allowing for the depth of batting facing them, with Chris Cowdrey due in at No. 8.

And that wicket should have come. Bob Woolmer completed a half-century of high quality before surviving two chances off consecutive balls from the unlucky Mike Hendrick. Barlow put down the first at slip, a difficult catch to his right. Woolmer edged again and this time, Bob Taylor dived across first slip but was unable to hang on to the ball – both uncharacteristic misses!

Mike Hendrick had done everything right; he was bowling majestically but nothing would stick. Had Woolmer gone when he had made 52 out of 82, it would have been a significant breach. Instead he went on to make 79 before, ironically, Hendrick caught him off Barlow – but at 117 for 4, Kent were almost there.

With Woolmer gone, Shepherd and captain Alan Ealham saw it through, giving Kent the Benson and Hedges Cup for the third time. Derbyshire were outplayed and though their achievement was to have reached the final, when the great day came, they flopped badly as they had in the Gillette Cup Final of 1969. The failure was essentially that of the batting. Only Peter Kirsten and Geoff Miller made contributions of any significance and both were out at the wrong time. Had either or both of them been able to see the innings through to its end, then it could have been a different story.

GOLD AWARD WINNER 1978 BOB WOOLMER

The son of a British business executive, Bob Woolmer was born in Kanpur, India, not far from the cricket ground. At the age of seven, he moved to England to begin his cricketing education at Yardley Court, Tonbridge, under the guidance of A.F. Brickmore, a former Kent player who was headmaster of the school. Woolmer, who later attended Skinners School, Tonbridge, took up a post as a sales representative with ICI in London but at the age of 20, he joined the Kent groundstaff. Later that summer he made his first-class debut against Essex and though he wasn't asked to bowl, he made an unbeaten half-century.

The following season he produced his best figures with the ball, taking 7 for 47 against Sussex at Canterbury. In 1970 he was awarded his county cap and at the end of the season, he spent the winter coaching in South Africa. It was here that he perfected his bowling armoury by learning to swing the ball away. In 1972 he picked up 13 wickets in the match with Sussex (6 for 70 and 7 for 65). In 1975 he performed the hat-trick for the MCC against the Australians at Lord's and later made his Test debut on the same ground. He was left out after his debut until the last match of the series at The Oval, scoring 149 – the slowest hundred ever made by an England batsman against Australia.

In 1976 he began to open the batting for Kent, scoring 1,461 runs at 56.19, capturing 50 wickets and holding four catches in an innings against Worcestershire to show his all-round talent. In 1977 he scored centuries against Australia at Lord's and Old Trafford. Including the Centenary Test, he had made seven appearances against the old enemy, scoring three hundreds. It equalled Peter May's record and was better than Grace, Graveney or Woolley!

Woolmer hit the highest score of his career, 203, against Sussex at Tunbridge Wells in 1982 before leaving the first-class scene two years later. A graceful right-handed batsman who scored 12,634 runs at 35.09 and useful medium-fast bowler who captured 334 wickets at 23.38 runs apiece, he later managed South Africa's national side to great success.

BENSON AND HEDGES CUP FINAL 1978

Played at Lord's, 22 July
Toss: Derbyshire
Result: Kent won by six wickets
Gold Award: Bob Woolmer
Adjudicator: Alec Bedser

DERBYSHIRE

				Fall of Wickets	
A. Hill	c Tavare b Jarvis	17		1st	11
A.J. Borrington	c Downton b Shepherd	0		2nd	32
P.N. Kirsten	c Shepherd b Asif Iqbal	41		3rd	33
E.J. Barlow	b Underwood	1		4th	88
G. Miller	b Shepherd	38		5th	121
H. Cartwright	c Ealham b Woolmer	12		6th	127
A.J. Harvey-Walker	b Shepherd	6		7th	127
R.W. Taylor	c Downton b Shepherd	0		8th	132
P.E. Russell	c Downton b Jarvis	4		9th	134
R.C. Wincer	not out	6		10th	147
M. Hendrick	run out	7			
Extras (lb 10 w 4 nb 1)		15			
Total (54.4 overs)		**147 all out**			

KENT

				Fall of Wickets	
R.A. Woolmer	c Hendrick b Barlow	79		1st	32
G.W. Johnson	c Barlow b Russell	16		2nd	34
C.J. Tavare	b Russell	0		3rd	70
Asif Iqbal	c Taylor b Russell	9		4th	117
A.G.E. Ealham	not out	23			
J.N. Shepherd	not out	19			
C.J.C. Rowe	did not bat				
C.S. Cowdrey	did not bat				
D.L. Underwood	did not bat				
P.R. Downton	did not bat				
K.B.S. Jarvis	did not bat				
Extras (lb 3 w 1 nb 1)		5			
Total (41.4 overs)		**151 for 4**			

KENT	O	M	R	W	DERBYSHIRE	O	M	R	W
Jarvis	9.4	3	19	2	Hendrick	11	2	23	0
Shepherd	11	2	25	4	Wincer	7	0	29	0
Underwood	11	3	21	1	Russell	11	2	28	3
Woolmer	10	2	15	1	Barlow	8.4	0	44	1
Asif Iqbal	8	1	26	1	Miller	2	0	8	0
Johnson	5	0	25	0	Kirsten	2	0	14	0

Umpires D.J. Constant and J.G. Langridge

1979
ESSEX v SURREY

When Essex won the Benson and Hedges Cup by beating Surrey by 35 runs, their success was the first honour of any kind which the county had won since its inception in 1876. When Essex were 172 for 1, it looked as though they were home and dry, but although they scored an impressive 290 for 6, an almost unassailable total in a 55-over game, Surrey made a very brave fight of it and got within 35 runs of this formidable target.

Essex skipper Keith Fletcher's acumen as one of the shrewdest captains in first-class cricket had obviously been a large factor in his side's challenges in the various competitions in recent years. He was up against another highly seasoned professional in Roger Knight. Though the Surrey captain did not have Fletcher's international experience, he was one of very few players to have been capped by three different counties – and he had won Benson and Hedges Gold Awards with each of them.

Surrey captain Roger Knight won the toss and put Essex in, despite the fact that he was missing the talents of West Indian pace bowler Sylvester Clarke from his attack. After the impressive Hugh Wilson had removed Mike Denness for 24, the aggressive South African Ken McEwan joined Graham Gooch. These two added 124 for the second wicket with McEwan's share being 72, an innings that included ten boundaries before he too fell to Wilson, courtesy of a Jack Richards' catch. This brought Essex captain Keith Fletcher to the crease but after hitting a stylish 34, he lost his off-stump to Surrey skipper Roger Knight.

Both Wilson and Knight were causing the Essex batsmen problems and Brian

Ken McEwan

Geoff Howarth

Hardie didn't last long, offering Intikhab Alam the simplest of chances. But Surrey had no answer to Graham Gooch, who was in imperious form. He went on to score a magnificent 120 – an innings that included three huge sixes as he recorded the first ever hundred in a Benson and Hedges Cup Final. Gooch became Hugh Wilson's fourth victim with the total on 273 for 5. Norbert Phillip gave the expensive Jackman his only wicket, but some lusty blows by Keith Pont took Essex's total to 290 for 6.

Surrey batsmen Alan Butcher and Monte Lynch struggled against the Essex opening attack of Lever and Phillip and it wasn't long before left-hander Butcher edged Lever to wicket-keeper Neil Smith. A change of bowling saw off-spinner Ray East replace Phillip and he dismissed Lynch with the score on 45. Surrey looked on the way out but New Zealand Test captain

Geoff Howarth and Surrey skipper Roger Knight pulled the innings together, and at 136 for 2 they were back in the hunt.

However, Essex all-rounder Keith Pont accounted for both of them – Knight edging to Neil Smith and Howarth finding Fletcher with the score on 187. David Smith was the next to go after a gutsy innings of 24, the first of Norbert Phillip's three victims, losing his off-stump to the West Indian all-rounder. Former England favourite Graham Roope tried to keep up the challenge with a hard-hitting innings of 39 not out but time proved to be the cardinal issue and wickets had to be surrendered in the chase for runs.

The tail was brushed aside as Intikhab Alam was caught by Pont off the bowling of Phillip and Surrey's last four batsmen were all clean bowled, all by different bowlers. John Lever's dismissal of Hugh Wilson in the gathering gloom meant that Essex had tasted success at last after over one hundred years of trying.

No other Benson and Hedges Final outcome had such lasting significance for the county involved, because it marked the beginning of a great era for Essex cricket under the guidance of first Keith Fletcher and later Graham Gooch. It was most appropriate, therefore, that former Essex favourite Trevor Bailey should be the one to hand the Gold Award to Graham Gooch.

The Essex squad, 1979

GOLD AWARD WINNER 1979
GRAHAM GOOCH

Graham Gooch made his Essex debut in 1973, hitting the first of 94 centuries for the county the following summer. He was soon seen as a very powerful and aggressive batsman and in 1975 was called into the Test side – albeit a little prematurely as he failed to score in either innings against the pace of Lillee and Thomson.

Though he retained his place for the next Test, he then disappeared from the international scene until 1978.

After his magnificent innings of 120 in the Benson and Hedges Final, he helped Essex win the 1979 County Championship.

The first of his 20 Test centuries came at Lord's against the West Indies in 1980, when he scored 123 out of the first 165 runs. In the Caribbean in 1980-81, he scored 116 at Bridgetown and 153 at Kingston to average 57.50 in the Test series. A year later he captained a rebel tour of South Africa and was banned from Test cricket for three years.

In 1982, Gooch hit 198 against Sussex in a Benson and Hedges zonal match – the highest score made in a one-day competition in England. The summer of 1984 was, without doubt, Gooch's best, when he established an Essex first-class record of 2,559 runs.

He returned to the England side in 1985 and hit 196 at The Oval as England won the series against Australia. He became captain of Essex in 1986 but despite leading the county to their third title in four years, he relinquished the post after a couple of seasons. He did, however, become captain of England and became a national hero when he led them to victory over the West Indies at Kingston in 1989-90. In 1990 he hit 154 as England beat New Zealand at Edgbaston and followed this with innings of 333 and 123 in the victory over India at Lord's. His triple century was the highest innings ever played by an England captain.

Capable of the destruction of any attack, Gooch lifted the spirits of English cricket by his own supreme example. When he retired from first-class cricket in 1997, he was both England's (8,900 runs at 42.58) and Essex's (30,701 runs at 51.77) leading run-getter of all time.

BENSON AND HEDGES CUP FINAL 1979

Played at Lord's, 21 July
Toss: Surrey
Result: Essex won by 35 runs
Gold Award: Graham Gooch
Adjudicator: Trevor Bailey

ESSEX

			Fall of Wickets	
M.H. Denness	c Smith b Wilson	24	1st	48
G.A. Gooch	b Wilson	120	2nd	172
K.S. McEwan	c Richards b Wilson	72	3rd	239
K.W.R. Fletcher	b Knight	34	4th	261
B.R. Hardie	c Intikhab Alam b Wilson	4	5th	273
K.R. Pont	not out	19	6th	276
N. Phillip	c Howarth b Jackman	2		
S. Turner	not out	1		
N. Smith	did not bat			
R.E. East	did not bat			
J.K. Lever	did not bat			
Extras (b 3 lb 8 w 1 nb 2)		14		
Total (55 overs)		**290 for 6**		

SURREY

			Fall of Wickets	
A.R. Butcher	c Smith b Lever	13	1st	21
M.A. Lynch	c McEwan b East	17	2nd	45
G.P. Howarth	c Fletcher b Pont	74	3rd	136
R.D.V. Knight	c Smith b Pont	52	4th	187
D.M. Smith	b Phillip	24	5th	205
G.R.J. Roope	not out	39	6th	219
Intikhab Alam	c Pont b Phillip	1	7th	220
R.D. Jackman	b East	1	8th	226
C.J. Richards	b Turner	1	9th	250
P.I. Pocock	b Phillip	7	10th	255
P.H.L. Wilson	b Lever	0		
Extras (b 4 lb 16 w 1 nb 3)		26		
Total (51.4 overs)		**255 all out**		

SURREY	O	M	R	W	ESSEX	O	M	R	W
Jackman	11	0	69	1	Lever	9.4	2	33	2
Wilson	11	1	56	4	Phillip	10	2	42	3
Knight	11	1	40	1	East	11	1	40	2
Intikhab Alam	11	0	38	0	Turner	11	1	47	1
Pocock	11	0	73	0	Pont	10	0	67	2

Umpires H.D. Bird and B.J. Meyer

1980
NORTHAMPTONSHIRE v ESSEX

Northamptonshire and Essex made Benson and Hedges Cup history when heavy overnight and morning rain left Lord's saturated and play for the day was abandoned. The final was played on the Monday after the Lord's groundstaff had done a magnificent job clearing the waterlogged outfield, and the square looked excellent considering the torrential pounding it had put up with during the past week. Sadly, the hallowed stadium was only half-full, many of the fans disappointed on Saturday being unable to return on Monday.

Northamptonshire skipper Jim Watts won the toss and elected to bat. Both Cook and Larkins played and missed against the Essex opening attack of Phillip and Lever. With the score on 17 and nine overs gone, Turner replaced Phillip at the Nursery End but it was Lever slanting the ball across the right-handers who continued to pose problems. Larkins hoisted Turner over mid-off but although the ball stopped short of the ropes on the damp outfield, the batsmen still managed to run four. Keith Pont replaced Lever at the Pavilion End but the England paceman had done a good job, conceding just seven runs off his six overs.

But with the score on 36, Essex broke through. Larkins tried to lift Pont over mid-on but got under it and Mike Denness ran back 15 yards to take a fine catch over his shoulder. Richard Williams started in spectacular style, cover and square driving Pont for a couple of superb boundaries to reach double figures in his first over. Just as the run rate had started to accelerate, Williams was out, caught at first slip by Ken McEwan as he tried to glance Pont down the leg-side. But Allan Lamb was immediately into his stride,

Keith Pont

Ian Lever

stroking Pont past square-leg for four. However, with the score on 78, Essex captured their third wicket when Cook edged Pont to Gooch at first slip.

An awful lot of Northamptonshire's hopes rested on Peter Willey and Allan Lamb. The pair were hitting the ball well enough but they could not pierce the well-placed Essex field. With the score on 110, Willey's frustration got the better of him as he tried to swing Turner through mid-wicket in the last over before lunch and was caught by McEwan running in from the boundary.

Northamptonshire's sad decline continued immediately after lunch when Jim Yardley was caught behind second ball as he tried to drive Gooch and thin-edged to wicket-keeper Neil Smith. The return of Keith Pont spelled the end of George Sharp as he was caught at point by Keith Fletcher off the first ball of the seamer's new spell. Lamb was itching for a big hit and it came when he smacked Lever into the tavern for six. Ray East hurt himself trying to take the catch.

Skipper Jim Watts scored 22 in a valuable partnership of 59 with Allan Lamb before being run out, while Lamb fell to a terrific diving catch at long-on by Brian Hardie for 72 as Northamptonshire totalled 209 – a score which did not look good enough to halt the batting might of Cup-holders Essex.

England opener Graham Gooch and South African Ken McEwan were making light work of the seamers following the dismissal of Denness as Essex cruised leisurely to 112 for 1 with 22 overs left.

But what a funny game cricket is – from the moment Gooch was gratefully grabbed at the second attempt by Allan Lamb at mid-on for 60 off his namesake Tim, Essex were in trouble. Off-spinner Peter Willey completed a brilliant spell of 2 for 34 by bowling danger-man McEwan six runs later. The South African was beaten by the turn as he shaped to cut and suddenly the whole complexion of the match had changed and Essex were 118 for 3 with two new batsmen in.

Determined to make this the best day of his career, Watts then bowled Hardie for nought and with Essex in trouble at 121 for 4, he pulled a masterstroke by bringing on spinner Richard Williams instead of another seamer.

Essex now needed six an over. Keith Pont charged down the wicket to Williams but George Sharp missed the leg-side stumping. Then Keith Fletcher slogged Watts to mid-wicket and was dropped by Allan Lamb. But Williams had the batsmen in all kinds of tangles and Pont, tied down ever since he came in, tried to rush the spinner again but the Welshman saw him coming and bowled him with a quicker one. Stuart Turner then lifted Watts into the tavern for six but Sarfraz returned and promptly had him caught at mid-on as he desperately tried to cross-bat the Pakistani down the ground.

Essex needed 47 off the last four overs, a seemingly impossible task, but Williams – who had bowled a brilliant seven overs for only 19 runs – was replaced by paceman Jim Griffiths. West Indian Norbert Phillip went berserk, smashing a giant six and a straight four, and 30 in all came from Griffiths's last 12 balls. In between Sarfraz bowled Fletcher but suddenly victory was possible and 11 were needed off the Pakistani's last over. But the big-hitting Phillip had lost the strike and Sarfraz was well able to cope with this sort of pressure situation and kept his cool to bowl Neil Smith with his second delivery. Essex would win if the scores were level and they were not all out, but despite a couple of twos, Northamptonshire survived the most gripping finale ever seen in a Lord's cup final to win the Benson and Hedges Cup by six runs.

GOLD AWARD WINNER 1980
ALLAN LAMB

When South African-born batsman Allan Lamb joined Northamptonshire in the summer of 1978, he had already been a regular in the Western Province Currie Cup side since 1972. Born of English parents, Lamb made his England debut almost immediately after becoming qualified by residence in 1982.

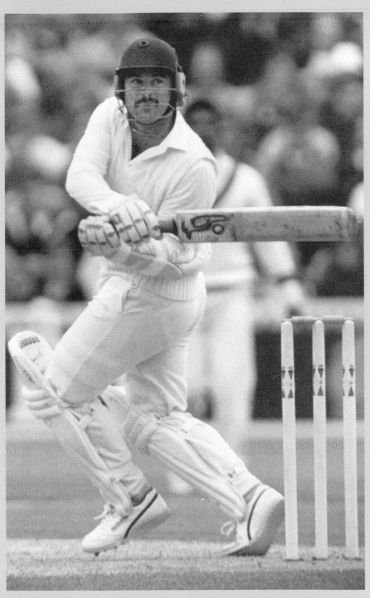

After hitting his maiden Test century against Sri Lanka in 1984, Lamb became the first batsman to achieve the feat of scoring hundreds in three successive Tests since Ken Barrington in 1967 in England's fight to shake off the utter dominance of Clive Lloyd's great West Indian side.

Lamb always seemed to reserve his best performances for the West Indies. Despite his form having lapsed, he was recalled to the England side in 1988 for the visit of the West Indies to his favourite ground, Lord's. As England chased a virtually impossible 442 for victory, Lamb kept the dream alive with a superb innings of 113, before being run out. Later in the series at Headingley, he astounded everyone by hobbling out to bat after tearing a calf muscle. Last seen on crutches, he defied the West Indies' pace attack for almost an hour and a half, batting on one leg!

In limited-overs internationals, where his powers of improvisation and fast, aggressive outfielding assumed great value, he scored 4,010 runs at an impressive average of 39.31.

Returning to the Union, Lamb promptly hit a career-best 294 against a strong Eastern Province side – winning 50,000 rand for sharing a record partnership of 355 and a further 15,000 rand for scoring 150 off fewer than 300 balls and 200 in under 400 balls.

Lamb became captain of Northamptonshire in 1989, leading them to success in the NatWest Trophy in 1992. He went on to score 32,502 runs at 48.94 before this joyful cricketer, a man who loves life to the full, parted company with the county.

BENSON AND HEDGES CUP FINAL 1980

Played at Lord's, 21 July
Toss: Northamptonshire
Result: Northamptonshire won by 6 runs
Gold Award: Allan Lamb
Adjudicator: Ken Barrington

NORTHAMPTONSHIRE

			Fall of Wickets	
G. Cook	c Gooch b Pont	29	1st	36
W. Larkins	c Denness b Pont	18	2nd	61
R.G. Williams	c McEwan b Pont	15	3rd	78
A.J. Lamb	c Hardie b Phillip	72	4th	110
P. Willey	c McEwan b Turner	15	5th	110
T.J. Yardley	c Smith b Gooch	0	6th	131
G. Sharp	c Fletcher b Pont	8	7th	190
P.J. Watts	run out	22	8th	193
Sarfraz Nawaz	not out	10	9th	209
T.M. Lamb	lbw b Turner	4	10th	209
B.J. Griffiths	b Turner	0		
Extras (b 1 lb 8 w 4 nb 3)		16		
Total (54.5 overs)		**209 all out**		

ESSEX

			Fall of Wickets	
M.H. Denness	b Willey	14	1st	52
G.A. Gooch	c A. Lamb b T. Lamb	60	2nd	112
K.S. McEwan	b Willey	38	3rd	118
K.W.R. Fletcher	b Sarfraz Nawaz	29	4th	121
B.R. Hardie	b Watts	0	5th	129
K.R. Pont	b Williams	2	6th	160
S. Turner	c Watts b Sarfraz Nawaz	16	7th	180
N. Phillip	not out	32	8th	198
N. Smith	b Sarfraz Nawaz	2		
R.E. East	not out	1		
J.K. Lever	did not bat			
Extras (b 1 lb 5 w 3)		9		
Total (55 overs)		**203 for 8**		

ESSEX	O	M	R	W
Lever	11	3	38	0
Phillip	11	1	38	1
Turner	10.5	2	33	3
Pont	11	1	60	4
Gooch	11	0	24	1

NORTHAMPTONSHIRE	O	M	R	W
Sarfraz Nawaz	11	3	23	3
Griffiths	7	0	46	0
Watts	8	1	30	1
T. Lamb	11	0	42	1
Willey	11	1	34	2
Williams	7	0	19	1

Umpires D.J. Constant and B.J. Meyer

1981

SURREY v SOMERSET

Though Surrey and Somerset were both very strong teams on paper, on the day there was only one team in it. Somerset possessing the world's greatest batsman in Viv Richards, the world's greatest bowler in Joel Garner and the world's greatest all-rounder in Ian Botham. They were streets ahead.

It was the vision of a packed Lord's that used to inspire the imagination of Viv Richards when he was a young boy in Antigua and it stirred the great man's genius again as Surrey's attack was torn apart. Two years earlier he had made England's World Cup Final attack look embarrassingly mundane as he scored an unbeaten 138, and followed it up later in the summer with 117 in the Gillette Cup Final victory over Northamptonshire. In 1980, he scored 145 in the Lord's Test, while this Benson and Hedges Final saw him score 132 not out. Somerset's other West Indian superstar, Joel Garner, also loved the home of cricket – World Cup Final, 5 for 38; Gillette Cup Final, 6 for 29; Lord's Test of 1980, 6 for 57; and this Benson and Hedges Final, 5 for 14.

These two outstanding individual performances not surprisingly left Surrey beaten in a one-day final for the third time in successive years. Having been put in to bat by Brian Rose, Surrey made a disastrous start, with Jack Richards being bowled by Garner, and Clinton tied down so much that when he hit Vic Marks into the safe hands of Peter Roebuck, Surrey were 16 for 2 off 16 overs! Knight and Howarth set about repairing the early damage and had taken the score to 63 when the New Zealander tried to hit Marks over the top but only succeeded in finding Roebuck, who took his second catch of the innings. There was a brief flurry from Monte Lynch with a quickfire 22 but he fell victim to Popplewell's slower ball. Garner then dismissed Smith and Clarke before finding the edge of Roger Knight's bat.

Without the Surrey captain's assertive innings of 92, burgeoning at a time when his side seemed not to know where the next run was coming from, there would have been no contest at all. A difficult batsman to bowl at, he used his long reach to drive either side of the wicket. Only once when he had made 9 did he give a chance, and that was a more or less impossible one to mid-on off Marks. The Somerset off-spinner deserved the best figures after Garner, giving the ball some air and collecting wickets at mid-off and mid-on. Dredge and Popplewell bowled steadily and the latter held a brilliant diving catch in the deep to dismiss Sylvester Clarke. Surrey's total of 194 for 8 was, thanks to Knight, a reasonable score, but it was felt that they had needed another 30 runs to exert greater pressure on their opponents.

However, their bowlers began well enough with Rose and Denning playing onto their stumps off Jackman and Clarke respectively. Surrey knew that if they were to win they would have to dismiss Viv Richards cheaply. Sylvester Clarke hurried and harried him, once rapping him on the arm and forcing Richards to call for a pain-killing spray. But Clarke bowled too

Roger Knight

few balls at the main target in his first spell and when he later returned for his second, his shoulders and his pace had dropped. In retrospect, perhaps Surrey's only hope was to have bowled Clarke for 11 fiery overs at the start.

But Richards got away, unbelievably adept as always at forcing the ball away between mid-wicket and mid-on, and Roebuck played second fiddle with good sense, scoring 22 in a third-wicket partnership of 105 before providing Roger Knight with a wicket. Botham succeeded him and without trying anything too outrageous thoroughly enjoyed himself with an innings of 37 not out. So, of course, did 'King Viv' whose unbeaten 132 was the highest individual innings in any Benson and Hedges Cup Final, while his team-mate Joel 'Big Bird' Garner's 5 for 14 was the second best bowling return in a final.

The West Countrymen strolled home with seven wickets and 10.3 overs to spare. There was never any doubt that Jim Laker would nominate Viv Richards for the Gold Award, even though Joel Garner probably felt hard done by!

Ian Botham

GOLD AWARD WINNER 1981
VIV RICHARDS

Viv Richards played his early cricket for his native Leeward Islands in the Caribbean's Shell Shield before joining Somerset in 1974. He soon benefited from the advice proffered by his county captain Brian Close, and in his first year in the West Country made over 1,000 first-class runs. He was constantly high in the English county averages, scoring over 1,000 runs every season until he was controversially released in 1986.

He enjoyed a vintage summer in 1977 when he scored 2,161 runs for an average of 65.48 and set a record for hitting the most sixes in the Sunday League with 26.

Along with Joel Garner, Richards catapulted Somerset to the centre of English cricket. In 1985, the Antiguan helped himself to a triple century off Warwickshire at Taunton. It was Richards' highest first-class score and the highest innings ever played for Somerset, coming off 258 balls with eight sixes and 42 fours. He hit eight other Championship centuries that summer and finished with an average of 76.50.

At Test level he was the surprise choice for the tour to India and Pakistan in 1974–75 but demonstrated his calibre immediately by scoring a match-winning 192 not out in the second Test at New Delhi. In eleven glorious Tests, beginning in Australia in 1976, the remarkable Antiguan scored 1,710 runs, ending the feat with a brilliant 291 at The Oval.

As he got older, Richards showed the ability to save his best performances for the big occasion. He relished Lord's, and in 1979 hit 138 in the World Cup Final to shatter the English bowling attack. He hit another century at Lord's, this time for Somerset in the Gillette Cup Final.

Richards, the first Leeward Islands' player to captain the West Indies, played in 121 Tests, scoring 8,540 runs at an average of 50.23. The only West Indian to score 100 first-class hundreds, he later had four seasons playing for Glamorgan, leading the Welsh county to the inaugural and multi-coloured AXA Equity and Law Sunday League.

BENSON AND HEDGES CUP FINAL 1981

Played at Lord's, 25 July
Toss: Somerset
Result: Somerset won by seven wickets
Gold Award: Viv Richards
Adjudicator: Jim Laker

SURREY

			Fall of Wickets	
G.S. Clinton	c Roebuck b Marks	6	1st	4
C.J. Richards	b Garner	1	2nd	16
R.D.V. Knight	c Taylor b Garner	92	3rd	63
G.P. Howarth	c Roebuck b Marks	16	4th	98
M.A. Lynch	c Garner b Popplewell	22	5th	132
D.M. Smith	b Garner	7	6th	166
S.T. Clarke	c Popplewell b Garner	15	7th	182
G.R.J. Roope	not out	14	8th	183
D.J. Thomas	b Garner	0		
R.D. Jackman	not out	2		
P.I. Pocock	did not bat			
Extras (b 2 lb 14 w 2 nb 1)		19		
Total (55 overs)		**194 for 8**		

SOMERSET

			Fall of Wickets	
B.C. Rose	b Jackman	5	1st	5
P.W. Denning	b Clarke	0	2nd	5
I.V.A. Richards	not out	132	3rd	110
P.M. Roebuck	c Smith b Knight	22		
I.T. Botham	not out	37		
N.F.M. Popplewell	did not bat			
V.J. Marks	did not bat			
D. Breakwell	did not bat			
J. Garner	did not bat			
D.J.S. Taylor	did not bat			
C.H. Dredge	did not bat			
Extras (nb 1)		1		
Total (44.3 overs)		**197 for 3**		

SOMERSET	O	M	R	W		SURREY	O	M	R	W
Garner	11	5	14	5		Clarke	8	1	24	1
Botham	11	2	44	0		Jackman	11	1	53	1
Dredge	11	0	48	0		Thomas	5.3	0	32	0
Marks	11	5	24	2		Pocock	11	1	46	0
Popplewell	11	0	45	1		Knight	9	0	41	0

Umpires H.D. Bird and B.J. Meyer

1982

NOTTINGHAMSHIRE v SOMERSET

Somerset became the first county to retain the Benson and Hedges Cup when they won this match comprehensively by nine wickets. Nottinghamshire, playing in their first one-day final, failed to make enough runs to make a match of it and so the result was academic long before the last rites were administered.

That Nottinghamshire, who were the reigning County Champions, were able to score only 130 was no fault of the pitch – admittedly the new ball did swing a little but then one would expect it to! The truth is that Nottinghamshire did not bat very well and perhaps the kindest assessment is that every team has an off day.

If Nottinghamshire were going to provide formidable opposition in the batting line-up, then it was likely to come from Derek Randall and Clive Rice, but Gold Award winner Vic Marks disposed of both of them when they were beginning to look potentially dangerous.

Somerset had won the toss and not surprisingly asked Nottinghamshire to bat. Joel Garner, without doubt the best bowler in a Benson and Hedges Final never to win a Gold Award, struck immediately, clean-bowling Paul Todd in his second over with his famous yorker that rocketed down at the batsman's feet from a great height. Garner used every inch of his height and the lift he extracted from what one would normally describe as a good length ball had all the batsmen in two minds.

Robinson and Randall grafted hard in adding 37 runs for the second wicket before the former fell to Colin Dredge, courtesy of a straightforward catch to Richards. Vic Marks then schemed out Randall, whose delight in stepping away to give himself room to cut had been duly noticed by the Somerset spinner. He pushed his second delivery through a little quicker and with a little more bounce and it left Randall, who had made 19, high and dry, the ball clipping the top of the leg-stump.

Basharat Hassan and Clive Rice then began to put bat to ball. They had added 46 runs for the fourth wicket when Dredge got one to move away down the hill and Hassan provided Derek Taylor with the first of two catches. Hallam Moseley then uprooted Birch's off-stump before Vic Marks bowled Clive Rice. Clive Rice had decided that the best way to deal with Marks was to hit him out of sight; the ploy was not a success as he missed the ball completely! However, he had played one or two superb shots in an innings of 27, which was to prove the top score for Nottinghamshire.

The Nottinghamshire innings then folded as Garner and Botham picked up a couple of wickets apiece. To start and finish an innings against Garner and Botham, with the mixture of Dredge, Moseley and Marks in between, is not a comforting thought for any batting side, but Nottinghamshire's total of 130 in just over 50 overs was the lowest recorded so far in the last round of this competition.

With Richard Hadlee well short of full fitness and Clive Rice not really wanting to bowl though he was forced into it, injury or no injury, Somerset's target was as easy as any Benson and Hedges Final had provided.

Richard Hadlee

Opener Peter Denning was caught by French off the bowling of Hendrick at 27 but that was to be Nottinghamshire's only success. Roebuck and Richards both made half-centuries, batting as if they were in the nets – it was as simple as that. Roebuck, who made an unbeaten 53, had added an extra dimension to his batting in the one-day game by steering the ball through the no-man's land where slips and gully would be on other days – it proved highly productive, with little or no risk attached. Viv Richards struck three resounding fours in one over from Hadlee before nonchalantly flicking away a leg-side delivery from Kevin Cooper to put Nottinghamshire out of their misery.

Somerset had won by nine wickets with nearly 22 overs to spare! It was a reflection of the day that the 'Man of the Match' took only two wickets and did not bat but Tom Graveney's choice of Vic Marks was absolutely right.

GOLD AWARD WINNER 1982
VIC MARKS

Vic Marks, whose technique developed in the back yard of his father's farm in Middle Chinnock, attended Blundell's School before going to Oxford University. An extremely dedicated and determined all-rounder, Marks was captain of the University side in the last two of his four summers as a blue. During his reign as captain, the University held the touring Australians to a draw in a two-day match. Marks as captain declared, setting the tourists a target of six runs an over to win – achievable but not inviting.

Though his bowling at times looked innocuous, he took some playing if the pitch gave him a little help. His long spells for Somerset helped him develop a control of flight which lured batsmen to their doom on good pitches. Marks's best figures were 8 for 17 against Lancashire at Bath in 1985, although he did take eight wickets in an innings on three occasions.

A competent middle-order batsman with an excellent temperament, his highest score for Somerset was 134 made against Worcestershire at Weston-super-Mare in 1984. Marks scored 1,000 runs in a season on two occasions and fell just 14 wickets short of completing the 'double' in 1984.

At Test level, Marks's last three scores were 83, 74 and 55 on the 1983–84 tour of Pakistan, while his 5 for 20 against New Zealand at Wellington during that same winter was for many years England's best bowling analysis in a limited-overs international.

Midway through his benefit season of 1988, Marks replaced his good friend Peter Roebuck as Somerset captain, leading the side with quiet authority. Marks, who scored 12,419 first-class runs at 30.29 and took 859 wickets at 33.28 runs apiece, eventually lost the incentive to continue as a player and gained notoriety as cricket correspondent of the *Observer* and *Test Match Special* commentator.

BENSON AND HEDGES CUP FINAL 1982

Played at Lord's, 24 July
Toss: Somerset
Result: Somerset won by nine wickets
Gold Award: Vic Marks
Adjudicator: Tom Graveney

NOTTINGHAMSHIRE

				Fall of Wickets	
P.A. Todd	b Garner	2		1st	3
R.T. Robinson	c Richards b Dredge	13		2nd	40
D.W. Randall	b Marks	19		3rd	40
S.B. Hassan	c Taylor b Dredge	26		4th	86
C.E.B. Rice	b Marks	27		5th	102
J.D. Birch	b Moseley	7		6th	106
R.J. Hadlee	b Garner	11		7th	122
B.N. French	c Taylor b Botham	8		8th	123
E.E. Hemmings	b Botham	1		9th	130
K.E. Cooper	b Garner	3		10th	130
M. Hendrick	not out	0			
Extras (lb 5 w 7 nb 1)		13			
Total (50.1 overs)		**130 all out**			

SOMERSET

				Fall of Wickets	
P.M. Roebuck	not out	53		1st	27
P.W. Denning	c French b Hendrick	22			
I.V.A. Richards	not out	51			
B.C. Rose	did not bat				
I.T. Botham	did not bat				
V.J. Marks	did not bat				
N.F.M. Popplewell	did not bat				
D.J.S. Taylor	did not bat				
J. Garner	did not bat				
C.H. Dredge	did not bat				
H.R. Moseley	did not bat				
Extras (b 5 w 1)		6			
Total (33.1 overs)		**132 for 1**			

SOMERSET	O	M	R	W		NOTTINGHAMSHIRE	O	M	R	W
Garner	8.1	1	13	3		Hadlee	9	0	37	0
Botham	9	3	19	2		Hendrick	8	0	26	1
Dredge	11	2	35	2		Cooper	5.1	0	41	0
Moseley	11	2	26	1		Rice	6	2	11	0
Marks	11	4	24	2		Hemmings	5	0	11	0

Umpires D.J. Constant and D.G.L. Evans

1983
MIDDLESEX v ESSEX

The record books will show that Middlesex won this Benson and Hedges Final and you cannot take credit away from a side that wins a cup, but it would be a little nearer to the mark to suggest that Essex threw it away. Middlesex kept pegging away when all hope seemed lost, and under this pressure Essex caved in – to the utter dismay of their followers.

This was a meeting of two teams who were both familiar with this most special of days. Essex intended to win the trophy for a second time and Middlesex were desperate to record their first success having narrowly lost to Leicestershire some eight years previously.

Neil Foster

Sent in to bat by Keith Fletcher, Middlesex had great trouble in coming to terms with the movement generated by what is their home pitch, as the ball seamed and swung in the hands of the Essex bowlers. Neil Foster dismissed both openers with 25 on the board, bowling Graham Barlow and having Wilf Slack, his first victim, caught at slip by Gooch. Mike Gatting, in his first season as Middlesex skipper, joined Radley and the two of them added 49 for the third wicket before Gatting was run out for 22. There had been no addition to the score when Keith Tomlins was adjudged leg-before to Graham Gooch, leaving Middlesex 74 for 4.

Emburey and Downton hit a few lusty blows but it was Clive Radley who held Middlesex's innings together. Edmonds and Williams both fell victim to Derek Pringle but Graham Gooch bowled his 11 overs for just 21 runs while Stuart Turner went for 24 and Neil Foster took three for

26. Clive Radley's 89 not out had been a typical fighting innings from a most determined cricketer and resulted in Middlesex reaching 196 for 8 from their allotted 55 overs.

It was almost 4 o'clock when Essex began their reply but they soon made up for lost time as Gooch and Hardie put bat to ball. The Essex openers had 79 on the board after just 11 overs before Gooch, who had been in majestic form, was caught behind off the bowling of Neil Williams. Ken McEwan then joined Scotsman Brian Hardie, and they took the score to 127 before McEwan's dismissal prompted a most dramatic turn of events. The South African batsman had made 34 runs in quickfire time when he flashed hard at Phil Edmonds and gave a difficult chance to Norman Cowans in the covers, which the Middlesex paceman snatched up.

Middlesex captain Mike Gatting then demonstrated that he had both the nerve and the knowledge to match his distinguished predecessor Mike Brearley by changing his bowlers astutely and marshalling his fields with great skill.

Brian Hardie

His opposite number Keith Fletcher was the next wicket to fall – Radley taking a bat-pad catch off Edmonds. Keith Pont then hit his own wicket after being hit on the head by a bouncer from Neil Williams; and anchorman Brian Hardie, one short of his half-century, edged a delivery from Cowans into the gloves of Paul Downton. Essex had lost four wickets for 29 runs in the space of 11 overs to a combination of aggressive pace bowling and cunning spin.

Yet Essex still had plenty of time and wickets in hand. Derek Pringle and Stuart Turner put their heads down and took the score up to 185. They were now just 12 runs short of victory, and with four overs to get them in and five wickets to fall they must have fancied their chances.

Then their world collapsed. Derek Pringle was leg-before to Wayne Daniel and Turner skied a catch to long-on which was well taken by substitute John Carr. Mike Gatting then held on to a tremendous catch from David East while Ray East was run out by the ever alert Radley. Norman Cowans settled the matter by bowling Neil Foster with the first ball of the last over to finish with 4 for 39. Essex's last five wickets had fallen for just seven runs in 19 balls!

Norman Cowans

GOLD AWARD WINNER 1983 CLIVE RADLEY

In the year that he left school, Clive Radley played under Bill Edrich in the Norfolk Minor Counties team. Bill was still associated with Middlesex and it was he who suggested that they should take young Radley on to their staff.

In 1965, only his second season with the county, he helped Fred Titmus add 277 for the sixth wicket against the South Africans at Lord's – his innings of 138 being taken from an attack that included Pollock, Barlow and Dumbrill.

As a batsman, Clive Radley was a most accomplished grafter of runs, with a fine temperament. His unorthodox batting style and ability to improvise put many a side in limited-overs games under great pressure. He scored centuries in all four competitions and hit hundreds off all the first-class counties.

After consistently scoring over 1,000 runs in a season, Radley was eventually elevated from county to Test status. He made eight appearances for his country, not once being on the losing side. He scored 481 runs at 48.10 with a highest score of 158 against New Zealand at Auckland. The innings lasted 648 minutes and was, at the time, the longest innings in New Zealand.

In the 1977 Gillette Cup Final against Glamorgan, he hit an unbeaten 85 to win the 'Man of the Match' award, and after another commanding innings of 89 against Essex in this 1983 Benson and Hedges Final, he scooped the award for a third time in a Lord's final with 67 in the 1984 NatWest Trophy Final as Middlesex won off the last ball.

The following summer against Northamptonshire at Uxbridge, he hit the first double-century of his career – he was 41 by now! His score of 200 contained a six, a five and 24 fours as he and Paul Downton added 289 for the fifth wicket.

Clive Radley had a benefit in 1977 and received a second one ten years later – not many players have done more to earn the 'double'! He was a magnificent team-man and the most effective of batsmen – few cricketers have given as much to the county of Middlesex or to the game of cricket itself.

BENSON AND HEDGES CUP FINAL 1983

Played at Lord's, 23 July
Toss: Essex
Result: Middlesex won by 4 runs
Gold Award: Clive Radley
Adjudicator: Les Ames

MIDDLESEX

				Fall of Wickets	
G.D. Barlow	b Foster	14		1st	10
W.N. Slack	c Gooch b Foster	1		2nd	25
C.T. Radley	not out	89		3rd	74
M.W. Gatting	run out	22		4th	74
K.P. Tomlins	lbw b Gooch	0		5th	123
J.E. Emburey	c D. East b Lever	17		6th	141
P.R. Downton	c Fletcher b Foster	10		7th	171
P.H. Edmonds	b Pringle	9		8th	191
N.F. Williams	c and b Pringle	13			
W.W. Daniel	not out	2			
Extras (b 3 lb 9 w 4 nb 3)		19			
Total (55 overs)		**196 for 8**			

ESSEX

				Fall of Wickets	
G.A. Gooch	c Downton b Williams	46		1st	79
B.R. Hardie	c Downton b Cowans	49		2nd	127
K.S. McEwan	c Cowans b Edmonds	34		3rd	135
K.W.R. Fletcher	c Radley b Edmonds	3		4th	151
K.R. Pont	hit wicket b Williams	7		5th	151
D.R. Pringle	lbw b Daniel	16		6th	185
S. Turner	c sub (Carr) b Cowans	9		7th	187
D.E. East	c Gatting b Cowans	5		8th	191
R.E. East	run out	0		9th	192
N.A. Foster	b Cowans	0		10th	192
J.K. Lever	not out	0			
Extras (lb 12 w 3 nb 8)		23			
Total (54.1 overs)		**192 all out**			

ESSEX	O	M	R	W		MIDDLESEX	O	M	R	W
Lever	11	1	52	1		Daniel	11	2	34	1
Foster	11	2	26	3		Cowans	10.1	0	39	4
Pringle	11	0	54	2		Williams	11	0	45	2
Turner	11	1	24	0		Emburey	11	3	17	0
Gooch	11	2	21	1		Edmonds	11	3	34	2

Umpires H.D. Bird and B.J. Meyer

1984

LANCASHIRE v WARWICKSHIRE

There were shades of the old Lancashire in this Benson and Hedges Final, bringing back fond memories of their golden days in the Gillette Cup when for three glorious years in succession they carried all before them. What is more, David Hughes and Jack Simmons, star performers of the early 1970s, still held the centre stage in this game. Although they had yet to win one single County Championship match this season, Lancashire had come to Lord's feeling that they had done the hardest part by beating Essex and Nottinghamshire on their home territory.

Warwickshire, asked to bat first, saw their first gamble fail when Paul Smith, promoted to opener, presented a simple catch to mid-on to Neil Fairbrother off Paul Allott without troubling the scorers. Alvin Kallicharran joined Dyer and they moved the total along to 48 at around 3 an over before Dyer was caught behind by former Warwickshire wicket-keeper Chris Maynard off Mike Watkinson. The Warwickshire opener's innings of 11 had taken almost an hour and a quarter! Meanwhile, the West Indian Test star reached his half-century in the 27th over with a four through mid-wicket off Steve O'Shaughnessy. It had come off 72 balls in 103 minutes and included seven boundaries.

At the halfway stage of their 55-over allocation, Warwickshire were 86 for 2 but Kallicharran brought up the 100 in the 30th over. Two runs later, there was a pre-lunch blow when Dennis Amiss tried to cut Watkinson and gave Maynard his second catch. Kallicharran went desperately close to being run out the ball before lunch when Geoff Humpage called for a quick single but fortunately for Warwickshire, the West Indian survived.

Warwickshire's early morning promise was wrecked in 72 disastrous minutes after lunch when they collapsed from a creditable 109 for 3 to an inexcusable 139 all out in the space of just 17.4 overs.

Neil Fairbrother

Paul Allott

Humpage gave Maynard his third catch of the innings before Anton Ferreira offered a simple caught-and-bowled chance to O'Shaughnessy.

The Lancashire all-rounder then bowled the big-hitting Chris Old to bring Asif Din to the crease. He had been included at the expense of either David Smith or Chris Lethbridge but he soon provided Steve Jefferies with his first wicket. The South African paceman then forced Kallicharran to hole out to Abrahams for a splendid 70, before dismissing Gladstone Small. Paul Allott brought Warwickshire's innings to a close when he dismissed Bob Willis.

Kallicharran's innings was so typical of his cricket this summer, scoring runs in profusion and with an ease which suggested that Lancashire's bowling was easy. It never was, as all five bowlers bowled well and with just reward. Paul Allott took 3 for 15, Jefferies three and Watkinson and O'Shaughnessy two each. Jack Simmons, although not taking a wicket, bowled

David Hughes

with his legendary meanness – 18 runs in 11 overs, nagging away with his low trajectory, floating an occasional one up a bit as if to offer bait, though the fish were not biting!

Warwickshire captain Bob Willis, making his last appearance for the county, soon removed England opener Graeme Fowler, but Lancashire then made steady progress despite the loss of Ormrod, until the fall of two quick wickets reduced them to 71 for 4. Another breakthrough then and Warwickshire just might have been in business. Lancashire's cause was helped by the unfortunate Gladstone Small, whose four overs included ten no-balls – and on top of that he finished with 0 for 30!

David Hughes and the young Neil Fairbrother then took a firm hold. Fairbrother looked so mature, in circumstances which could have been a trifle unnerving for anyone, and he played some fine shots, giving the textbook answer to anything short. He also drove and cut well, making the result academic – Lancashire won by six wickets with more than 12 overs to spare.

Peter May awarded the £500 'Man of the Match' award to Lancashire captain John Abrahams. May said it was for the way Abrahams had led his side. It certainly could not have been for the individual performance as he did not bowl and was the only Lancashire batsman to get a duck!

GOLD AWARD WINNER 1984
JOHN ABRAHAMS

John Abrahams came to England from Cape Town with his parents in the early 1960s. His father Cec, a fine cricketer himself, joined Milnrow in the Central Lancashire League. It wasn't too long before the pair were facing each other in a League game, for although John was batting in the middle order for Milnrow, his father had by then become Rochdale's professional.

The young Abrahams, who was a left-hand batsman and off-break bowler, soon attracted Lancashire's attention, and because of his tremendous fielding ability, often appeared quite regularly as a substitute fielder in the county's one-day games.

Though he had made his first-class debut for Lancashire in 1973, it was another four years before he won a regular place in the side. That summer of 1977 also saw him score the first of 14 centuries for the county, when he made an unbeaten 101 in the Roses match at Old Trafford. It was another five years before he was awarded his county cap, this being the first season he had succeeded in passing 1,000 runs.

In 1983 he deputised for Clive Lloyd as Lancashire captain on a number of occasions before being appointed on a permanent basis the following summer. He showed that the captaincy hadn't affected his batting, scoring a career-best unbeaten 201 against Warwickshire at Nuneaton.

He remained Lancashire's captain for the 1985 season and though he played in every match in the County Championship, and in all the one-day competitions, the committee reinstated Clive Lloyd for the summer of 1986. John Abrahams responded magnificently, scoring 1,251 runs at 40.35. Following a well-deserved testimonial in 1988, Abrahams, who had scored 9,980 runs for Lancashire at 29.70, parted company with the county club he had served for fifteen years.

After playing minor county cricket for Shropshire, John became Heywood's professional in the same Central Lancashire League that he had graced in his early days.

BENSON AND HEDGES CUP FINAL 1984

Played at Lord's, 21 July
Toss: Lancashire
Result: Lancashire won by six wickets
Gold Award: John Abrahams
Adjudicator: Peter May

WARWICKSHIRE

			Fall of Wickets	
R.I.H.B. Dyer	c Maynard b Watkinson	11	1st	1
P.A. Smith	c Fairbrother b Allott	0	2nd	48
A.I. Kallicharran	c Abrahams b Jefferies	70	3rd	102
D.L. Amiss	c Maynard b Watkinson	20	4th	115
G.W. Humpage	c Maynard b Allott	8	5th	121
A.M. Ferreira	c and b O'Shaughnessy	4	6th	127
C.M. Old	b O'Shaughnessy	5	7th	132
Asif Din	c Ormrod b Jefferies	3	8th	133
G.C. Small	lbw b Jefferies	2	9th	134
N. Gifford	not out	2	10th	139
R.G.D. Willis	c Jefferies b Allott	2		
Extras (lb 4 nb 8)		12		
Total (50.4 overs)		**139 all out**		

LANCASHIRE

			Fall of Wickets	
G. Fowler	c Humpage b Willis	7	1st	23
J.A. Ormrod	c Humpage b Ferreira	24	2nd	43
S.J. O'Shaughnessy	c Humpage b Ferreira	22	3rd	70
D.P. Hughes	not out	35	4th	71
J. Abrahams	c Humpage b Smith	0		
N.H. Fairbrother	not out	36		
S.T. Jefferies	did not bat			
J. Simmons	did not bat			
C. Maynard	did not bat			
M. Watkinson	did not bat			
P.J.W. Allott	did not bat			
Extras (lb 6 w 1 nb 9)		16		
Total (42.4 overs)		**140 for 4**		

LANCASHIRE	O	M	R	W	WARWICKSHIRE	O	M	R	W
Allott	8.4	0	15	3	Willis	9	0	19	1
Jefferies	11	2	28	3	Small	4	0	30	0
Watkinson	9	0	23	2	Ferreira	11	2	26	2
O'Shaughnessy	11	1	43	2	Old	10.4	3	23	0
Simmons	11	3	18	0	Smith	6	0	20	1
					Gifford	2	1	6	0

Umpires D.J. Constant and D.G.L. Evans

1985

ESSEX v LEICESTERSHIRE

Victory for Leicestershire over the more fancied Essex gave them their third success in the competition that they had won in its inaugural year of 1972, and in doing so they made the highest score by a side batting second in the Benson and Hedges Final.

Essex suffered a setback when skipper Keith Fletcher was ruled out with a side strain. He was replaced by Alan Lilley, with Gooch taking over as captain. The England opener was soon in action after Leicestershire skipper David Gower won the toss and put Essex in on a pleasant morning, but with a poor weather forecast for later in the day, there was the unfortunate prospect of the match being carried over to Monday.

Gooch made an impressive start by scoring six of the seven runs from Agnew's opening over but shortly afterwards, a short sharp shower drove the players off. When the players returned, the game resumed in bright sunshine! Gooch and Hardie got themselves into a tangle when Parsons made a good stop at mid-off but by the time the fielder had regained his feet, the run-out chance had gone. Leicestershire's bowling was tight with Les Taylor coming off after bowling five overs for five runs. Parsons and Clift were also economical before Willey joined the attack with Essex 58 for 0 from 21 overs.

The score had risen to 65 with Gooch on 36 when he advanced down the pitch to drive Willey, missed and Garnham made a hash of what should have been a routine stumping. Six runs later the first wicket did go down when Clift, who had produced the occasional fine delivery, was driven hard and straight by Hardie and the bowler leapt high to take a brilliant overhead return catch. In the 34th over, with the Essex score on 101, Willey, having just seen a full toss dispatched to the cover boundary by Gooch, got his revenge with the next

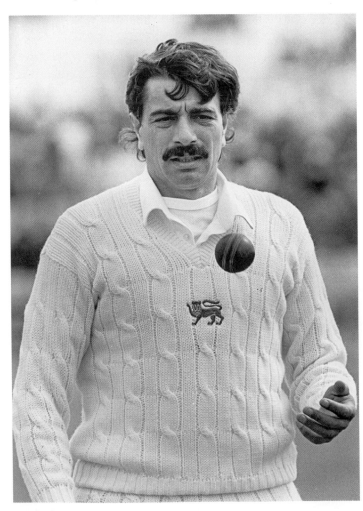

Les Taylor

David Gower

ball. Gooch tried to make extra room to drive through the off-side, missed and was bowled. Parsons had bad luck the following over when McEwan edged just short of the diving Garnham.

Essex had reached 147 for 2 when Les Taylor's persistent accuracy was rewarded with three good wickets – Paul Prichard, Ken McEwan and Derek Pringle – for 6 in just 15 balls. Then Jonathan Agnew and Paddy Clift demonstrated the virtue of bowling straight, dismissing Lilley and Gladwin respectively. Chris Balderstone then shed about twenty years to run out Stuart Turner, another member of cricket's exclusive over-40s club!

In spite of the record books, Essex's total of 213 for 8 did not look like being enough but Leicestershire made a poor start – Chris Balderstone mistiming a pull to mid-wicket, and Ian Butcher falling to a sparkling low catch by Paul Prichard at wide mid-on.

That left Leicestershire at 37 for 2 but a partnership of 83 in 17 overs between Willey and David Gower swung the pendulum again. Gower played some magnificent shots – one cover drive off the bowling of Derek Pringle will take a long time to fade from the memory – but just before the tea interval, he failed to get over a rising ball from Neil Foster and was brilliantly caught by Alan Lilley at point.

Soon after the interval, Whitaker and Briers both paid the penalty for not getting properly forward to Gooch's deceptive swing bowling, and all of a sudden Leicestershire were wobbling at 135 for 5. They had lost three wickets for only 15 runs and no one with Leicestershire affiliations needed reminding that their team had never managed, batting second, to score more than 194 and win a one-day final in the fourteen years of the competition so far.

But then Peter Willey, at times quite ferocious off his legs, was joined by Mike Garnham. Plundering anything short of a length, the two of them simply took the Essex seam attack apart and Leicestershire had 18 deliveries to spare when Garnham – with the pavilion clock showing 7.40 p.m. – drove John Lever straight back for the winning boundary.

'Man of the Match' was 35-year-old Peter Willey, who played one of the most valuable innings seen in a one-day final. The Leicestershire vice-captain was a long time getting his eye in and only got into double figures after facing 32 deliveries. But he battered 18 more runs off the next nine balls he faced and, once he found a partner, a difficult target of 79 off the final 15 overs on a slow pitch was knocked off in style.

The underdogs certainly didn't 'freeze' on the big day – any semblance of nervous tension disappearing during the lunch interval, when amid much hilarity, part of the dressing-room ceiling came away and landed on Jonathan Agnew's head!

GOLD AWARD WINNER 1985
PETER WILLEY

Peter Willey began his career as a fast-bowling all-rounder but knee trouble forced him to slow down and to his rugged batsmanship he added a crisp off-spinner, bowled with a muscular arm after a short, unelaborate run-up. He made his debut for Northamptonshire in 1966, against Cambridge University, aged just 16 years 180 days, scoring an unbeaten 78 in the second innings.

Over the years, his innate toughness and natural gift of timing equipped him ideally for dealing with the fastest bowling, especially against the ferocious West Indian attack. Immensely strong off the back foot, he was also instantly recognisable at the crease from a vast distance because his stance was so extraordinarily square-on that he looked as if he was facing a bowler about to deliver from square-leg. Miraculously, he always had time to move into the right position to play his off-side strokes.

Willey's highest first-class score was 227 against Somerset at Northampton in 1976, while at Test level, he managed two centuries, including a best of 102 against the West Indies at St John's on the 1980–81 tour of the Caribbean. His other century had come the previous summer also against the West Indies at The Oval. Willey who scored 100 not out, shared in a match-saving tenth-wicket unbeaten stand of 117 with Bob Willis – England's third ever tenth-wicket century stand. He scored 1,000 runs in a season on ten occasions, with a best of 1,783 at an average of 50.94 in 1982.

Willey left Northamptonshire after 18 years, having faded from the Test scene under the politically-inspired ban because he toured South Africa, and joined Leicestershire in readiness for the 1984 season. During his first summer at Grace Road, he shared in the county's fourth-wicket record unbroken stand of 290 with Tim Boon against Warwickshire. In 1987 he was appointed captain but after just one unhappy season, he relinquished the post.

Willey played for Leicestershire until 1991, taking his total of first-class runs to 24,361 at 30.56 and his tally of wickets to 756 at 30.95 runs apiece. He later umpired on the county circuit and at the time of writing has officiated in twenty-four Tests.

BENSON AND HEDGES CUP FINAL 1985

Played at Lord's, 20 July
Toss: Leicestershire
Result: Leicestershire won by five wickets
Gold Award: Peter Willey
Adjudicator: Denis Compton

ESSEX

				Fall of Wickets	
G.A. Gooch	b Willey	57		1st	71
B.R. Hardie	c and b Clift	25		2nd	101
P.J. Prichard	b Taylor	32		3rd	147
K.S. McEwan	c Garnham b Taylor	29		4th	163
D.R. Pringle	c Agnew b Taylor	10		5th	164
C. Gladwin	b Clift	14		6th	191
A.W. Lilley	b Agnew	12		7th	195
D.E. East	not out	7		8th	198
S. Turner	run out	3			
N.A. Foster	not out	6			
J.K. Lever	did not bat				
Extras (b 1 lb 15 w 1 nb 1)		18			
Total (55 overs)		**213 for 8**			

LEICESTERSHIRE

				Fall of Wickets	
J.C. Balderstone	c Prichard b Pringle	12		1st	33
I.P. Butcher	c Prichard b Turner	19		2nd	37
D.I. Gower	c Lilley b Foster	43		3rd	120
P. Willey	not out	86		4th	123
J.J. Whitaker	b Gooch	1		5th	135
N.E. Briers	lbw b Gooch	6			
M.A. Garnham	not out	34			
P.B. Clift	did not bat				
G.J. Parsons	did not bat				
J.P. Agnew	did not bat				
L.B. Taylor	did not bat				
Extras (b 2 lb 9 w 2 nb 1)		14			
Total (52 overs)		**215 for 5**			

LEICESTERSHIRE	O	M	R	W	ESSEX	O	M	R	W
Agnew	11	1	51	1	Lever	11	0	50	0
Taylor	11	3	26	3	Foster	11	2	32	1
Parsons	11	0	39	0	Pringle	10	0	42	1
Clift	11	1	40	2	Turner	10	1	40	1
Willey	11	0	41	1	Gooch	10	1	40	2

Umpires H.D. Bird and K.E. Palmer

1986
KENT v MIDDLESEX

In a desperate finish amid heavy rain and appalling light, Middlesex won the Benson and Hedges Cup by two runs in what was the closest, and at its climax, the most exciting of finals. As on the last time these two sides met, in the final of the NatWest Trophy, which Middlesex also won off the last ball, their heroes were John Emburey and Clive Radley.

Though Emburey was named 'Man of the Match', the man who made the match was Kent's Graham Cowdrey. Coming in at 62 for 4, chasing a target of 200 for victory, he steadied and then, together with Baptiste and Ellison, lifted Kent's reply, hitting Edmonds for a couple of sixes into the Grandstand. When he was finally out in the 53rd over, Kent were 178 for 7. With 51 needed off five overs, Kent's hopes were still slim but Marsh, Ellison and Dilley continued the onslaught and when the Kent wicket-keeper hit Hughes for six off the third ball of the final over, only six were needed for an historic victory. But in their third consecutive last ball final, Middlesex's nerve held. Dilley was left with five to get off the last delivery but with the crowd pouring onto the field and the rain pouring down, he could only manage a two.

It was no surprise that Chris Cowdrey should put Middlesex in on a grey overcast day. The conditions were ideal for the seam and swing bowlers but Kent had left Terry Alderman in the pavilion, preferring the all-rounder Eldine Baptiste.

Graham Dilley was too fast and straight for Slack, who lost his middle stump without getting off the mark. Andy Miller and Mike Gatting set about repairing the damage, treating the bowling with the caution it deserved. By now, Richard Ellison had begun a beautiful spell of swing bowling from the Nursery End, which eventually

Richard Ellison

Graham Dilley

brought success when Gatting and Butcher touched successive out-swingers to Marsh, who took the first of his three catches low to his right and the second by his chest, an indication of the pitch's uneven bounce.

Middlesex were now 66 for 3 and only 11 runs came off the next 10 overs as Radley and Miller struggled for control. Chris Cowdrey brought himself on, Miller dabbled once too often outside the off-stump and Marsh took his third catch.

After lunch, Radley and Downton took 29 off the first four overs before the former, appearing in his seventh cup final, was run out by Marsh. A few unorthodox shots from Emburey and some more cultured strokes from Edmonds and Hughes left Middlesex one short of 200, leaving Kent a target of 3.6 an over.

Kent started disastrously with Mark Benson edging Cowans to Downton. Wayne Daniel bowled with great hostility off a short run-up and Tavare was put out of his misery, giving

Graham Cowdrey

the Middlesex wicket-keeper his second catch. Simon Hinks, who had been playing with rather more determination, was leg-before to Cowans and Kent were 20 for 3. Taylor and Chris Cowdrey were beginning to repair the damage when Hughes got one to lift and leave the Kent skipper and Emburey took a brilliant reflex catch to his right at slip. It was a vital breakthrough, reducing Kent to 62 for 4. The nine overs before tea cost just nine runs and Emburey, finding Taylor unwilling to use his feet, bowled his first six overs for just five runs!

After Taylor had played an ill-judged shot to deep mid-on, the arrival of Eldine Baptiste brought an urgency to the Kent innings. Graham Cowdrey proved a willing accomplice as the two snatched and grabbed any runs they could off the Middlesex spinners.

After Cowdrey had lifted Edmonds into the Grandstand for six, Daniel was brought back to try and stem the flow. Cowdrey and Baptiste deflected and swung with profitable results. Wayne Daniel's last four overs went for 33 as Cowdrey completed a masterly and courageous half-century. When Baptiste was bowled by Edmonds, the two had added 69 in a dozen overs. This brought Richard Ellison to the wicket and he promptly lofted Simon Hughes for a massive straight six.

Cowdrey's gallant innings ended with a catch to Radley at mid-wicket and Ellison followed soon after, bowled by Edmonds in the game's penultimate over. The rain increased and the light darkened as Marsh and Dilley flailed but failed. A bedraggled Mike Gatting lifted the cup to maintain a remarkable sequence – Middlesex had won a trophy in each of their last five years.

John Emburey's all-round contribution of defensive slow bowling, pragmatic innings of 28 and brilliant slip catch earned him the Gold Award nomination from David Gower.

GOLD AWARD WINNER 1986
JOHN EMBUREY

John Emburey had toured Canada with Surrey Young Cricketers and was desperately keen to join his native county. However, a letter from Surrey coach Arthur McIntyre brought great disappointment, for the county already had three spinners on the staff. McIntyre suggested he try Middlesex, which he did, but in his first six seasons on the staff, he played in just a handful of games, due to the presence of Fred Titmus. Nonetheless, Emburey's six-year apprenticeship went a long way in helping his first full season to be a great success as he took 81 wickets.

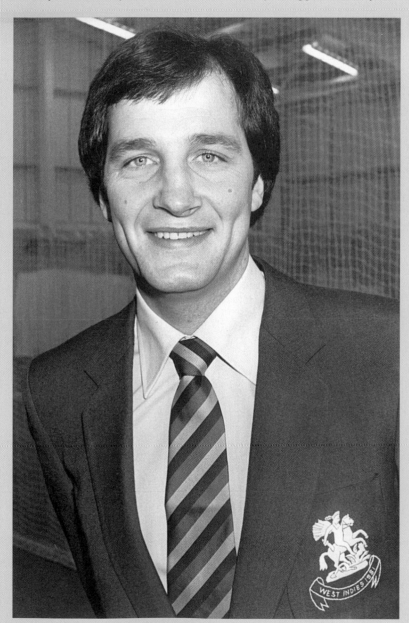

Emburey made his international debut in the final test of 1978 against New Zealand, dismissing Bruce Edgar with his fourth ball, and over the next few years he emerged as one of the world's leading off-spinners. He played in 64 Tests for England, his greatest performance coming in the Ashes series of 1986–87. The Ashes had been safely retained when the two teams came together at Sydney for the final Test. Australia had scored 343 in their first innings and England were 142 for 6 when Emburey, hobbling with a groin strain, came out to bat.

He stayed at the crease for three-and-a-half hours and scored 69 to keep England in the hunt. Then came his greatest contribution in a Test match as he bowled 46 overs of controlled spin bowling to take 7 for 78. England needed 320 to win and though Gatting made a brave 96 and Emburey stayed more than an hour for his 22, he was beaten by a grubber with just one over remaining! Also on that tour, Emburey established a world record by scoring 46 entirely in boundaries for an England XI against Tasmania at Hobart.

After 23 seasons with Middlesex in which he took 1,430 wickets, Emburey had a couple of seasons with Northamptonshire, combining playing with his duties as the county's coach.

BENSON AND HEDGES CUP FINAL 1986
Played at Lord's, 12 July
Toss: Kent
Result: Middlesex won by 2 runs
Gold Award: John Emburey
Adjudicator: David Gower

MIDDLESEX

				Fall of Wickets	
W.N. Slack	b Dilley		0	1st	6
A.J.T. Miller	c Marsh b C. Cowdrey		37	2nd	66
M.W. Gatting	c Marsh b Ellison		25	3rd	66
R.O. Butcher	c Marsh b Ellison		0	4th	85
C.T. Radley	run out		54	5th	151
P.R. Downton	lbw b Ellison		13	6th	163
J.E. Emburey	b Baptiste		28	7th	183
P.H. Edmonds	not out		15		
S.P. Hughes	not out		4		
N.G. Cowans	did not bat				
W.W. Daniel	did not bat				
Extras (lb 8 w 11 nb 4)			23		
Total (55 overs)		**199 for 7**			

KENT

				Fall of Wickets	
M.R. Benson	c Downton b Cowans		1	1st	17
S.G. Hinks	lbw b Cowans		13	2nd	20
C.J. Tavare	c Downton b Daniel		3	3rd	20
N.R. Taylor	c Miller b Edmonds		19	4th	62
C.S. Cowdrey	c Emburey b Hughes		19	5th	72
G.R. Cowdrey	c Radley b Hughes		58	6th	141
E.A.E. Baptiste	b Edmonds		20	7th	178
R.M. Ellison	b Edmonds		29	8th	182
S.A. Marsh	not out		14		
G.R. Dilley	not out		4		
D.L. Underwood	did not bat				
Extras (lb 9 w 8)			17		
Total (55 overs)		**197 for 8**			

KENT	O	M	R	W	MIDDLESEX	O	M	R	W
Dilley	11	2	19	1	Cowans	9	2	18	2
Baptiste	11	0	61	1	Daniel	11	1	43	1
C.S. Cowdrey	11	0	48	1	Gatting	4	0	18	0
Ellison	11	2	27	3	Hughes	9	2	35	2
Underwood	11	4	36	0	Emburey	11	5	16	0
					Edmonds	11	1	58	3

Umpires D.J. Constant and D.R. Shepherd

1987

NORTHAMPTONSHIRE v YORKSHIRE

J im Love steered Yorkshire to a famous victory over Northamptonshire, when with just one delivery left and the scores level at 244, he calmly blocked the last ball bowled by Winston Davis to clinch the match on the fewer wickets down rule. It was a traditionally nail-biting finish to a highly competitive and thoroughly entertaining game of cricket. For Northamptonshire though, it was a tragic repeat of their last appearance in a Lord's cup final six years earlier, when they lost the NatWest Trophy to Derbyshire on the same rule!

The New Mound Stand at Lord's, complete with benefactor John Paul Getty, awaited its proper christening at last with the promise of a full day's cricket between two of the in-form teams of the day. Phil Carrick won the toss and put Northamptonshire in to bat, hoping to make the most of any early morning moisture.

Openers Geoff Cook and Wayne Larkins found Paul Jarvis quite a handful. Fast, with impressive line and length, he had Cook snapped up at short leg by Blakey in only his second over with one that lifted. Ten overs later, Larkins, busily accumulating runs, got a leading edge when trying to work a ball from Peter Hartley and gave a steepling catch to Carrick in the covers. Allan Lamb arrived at the wicket and got on with the job immediately with customary deft glances and sharp singles. Rob Bailey, who had been hitting the ball with imperious ferocity, flashed once too often at a wide delivery. He edged it and Martyn Moxon flung himself full-length to his right to take a marvellous catch. David Capel joined

David Capel

Richard Williams

Lamb but after the pair had added 44, Jarvis was recalled into the attack and forced Lamb to bottom-edge a catch to the diving Bairstow.

Northamptonshire were now in trouble on 92 for 4. Phil Carrick then put the brakes on with a miserly spell of 11 overs for 30 runs. Northamptonshire, with Capel and Williams having to graft for their runs, went in to lunch at 128 for 4 with 19 overs remaining.

During the afternoon, Capel and Williams set about the Yorkshire attack in a positive manner. Capel brought up his half-century, scored off 67 balls, with a scorching drive to the extra-cover boundary. His fifth-wicket partnership with all-rounder Williams added 120 in 28 overs and they ensured that Yorkshire would be set a target beyond the reach of any side batting second in a previous domestic final.

With five overs remaining, Jarvis got one to nip back and Williams, trying to run it down to third man, got an edge to Bairstow. The Yorkshire pace bowler then spread-eagled Wild's stumps before Capel going for another extravagant drive off Hartley, got an inside edge onto his stumps, just three runs short of what would have been a thoroughly deserved hundred. An innings of the highest order, it was the cornerstone of Northamptonshire's highly respectable final total of 244 for 7.

Facing a required run rate of 4.45 per over, Moxon and Metcalfe gave Yorkshire a good start, though the latter was fortunate that the brilliant leg-side catch by Ripley off his edge from Davis was a no-ball. The West Indian was bowling far too short and Walker was too ragged. Capel soon replaced Walker but he appeared tired after his marathon innings. After 20 overs and with Yorkshire 83 for no wicket, Geoff Cook turned to Richard Williams to work in harness with Nick Cook, hoping that his spinners could unlock the White Rose county's stronghold. Three overs later, Cook beat Moxon in the flight and he was bowled for 45. As so often happens with good partnerships, both openers were to depart in quick succession. Williams bowled a full toss to Metcalfe, who, with great precision, picked out Winston Davis in front of the Tavern. Yorkshire were now 101 for 2 after 28 overs, just as Northamptonshire had been at the same stage.

In the next over, Williams bowled a long-hop and Blakey too spooned the ball into the deep for Davis to take another catch. Yorkshire had lost three wickets for six runs – Kevin Sharp and Jim Love had a tense uphill battle on their hands. With Davis and Williams operating, they found runs hard to come by and the run rate crept up to seven. Love, confident in the knowledge that he had yet to be dismissed in the competition this season, began to cut loose but Sharp provided Williams with his third wicket, chopping his last delivery onto his stumps.

Love was then joined by the ebullient David Bairstow, and the two set about the Northamptonshire attack. Young Duncan Wild, who strangely was not asked to bowl, made two outstanding boundary saves in front of the Tavern area. With just 23 needed for victory, Bairstow drove the ball back hard at Walker, who dived to his left, deflecting it to Bailey, who then calmly threw it to Ripley. Having started to run, Bairstow turned and dived for his crease but he was out of his ground. Phil Carrick then joined Love but he too was run out, sacrificing himself in the 54th over.

Although Rob Bailey's short underarm throw off the penultimate ball of the match should have hit the stumps and run out Sidebottom, thus requiring Yorkshire to score off the last ball of the match to win, Yorkshire had done enough. Jim Love's unbeaten 75 duly won him the Gold Award from adjudicator Mike Gatting.

GOLD AWARD WINNER 1987
JIM LOVE

Jim Love's beginnings with Yorkshire were not all that auspicious. He played a few games for the county in 1975, after scoring 95 at Harrogate for D.H. Robbin's XI against Yorkshire, but his average from five matches was 9.16, and a maiden century the following season did not blind him to the fact that earning a regular place in the Yorkshire side seemed to be no easier task than in the old days.

He scored his superb 163 against Nottinghamshire at Bradford: Lumb was soon out and Love, at No. 3, was in effect opening with Boycott. He had a fine season in 1976 but his progress was irregular and a few years later when he hit his career-best score of 170 not out against Worcestershire at New Road, he was promptly dropped!

A winter spent in Australia certainly contributed to his development but an earlier visit to South Africa had not impressed him quite so much and it ended in an early return to England, following an understandable attack of homesickness.

The rich promise of his early years was allied to maturing judgement and the elimination of non-profit-making strokes such as the lap and the sweep which needed to be reserved for special situations and the one-day game.

Love played for England in three limited-overs internationals against Australia, scoring 43 in the second of these. He was at his best in the Benson and Hedges Cup where he scored 1,113 runs at 41.22, while at county level he passed 1,000 runs in a season on two occasions with a best of 1,203 in 1981.

Quietly spoken, personable and articulate, Jim Love was not a typical Yorkshire professional cricketer of the old school and after scoring 10,327 first-class runs at 31.10, he moved into Minor County cricket with Lincolnshire.

BENSON AND HEDGES CUP FINAL 1987

Played at Lord's, 11 July
Toss: Yorkshire
Result: Yorkshire won by losing fewer wickets
Gold Award: Jim Love
Adjudicator: Mike Gatting

NORTHAMPTONSHIRE

			Fall of Wickets	
G. Cook	c Blakey b Jarvis	1	1st	3
W. Larkins	c Carrick b Hartley	15	2nd	31
R.J. Bailey	c Moxon b Fletcher	26	3rd	48
A.J. Lamb	c Bairstow b Jarvis	28	4th	92
D.J. Capel	b Hartley	97	5th	212
R.G. Williams	c Bairstow b Jarvis	44	6th	226
D.J. Wild	b Jarvis	6	7th	232
W.W. Davis	not out	10		
D. Ripley	not out	6		
N.G.B. Cook	did not bat			
A. Walker	did not bat			
Extras (b 2 lb 3 w 2 nb 4)		11		
Total (55 overs)		**244 for 7**		

YORKSHIRE

			Fall of Wickets	
M.D. Moxon	b N. Cook	45	1st	97
A.A. Metcalfe	c Davis b Williams	47	2nd	101
R.J. Blakey	c Davis b Williams	1	3rd	103
K. Sharp	b Williams	24	4th	160
J.D. Love	not out	75	5th	223
D.J. Bairstow	run out	24	6th	235
P. Carrick	run out	10		
A. Sidebottom	not out	2		
P.J. Hartley	did not bat			
P.W. Jarvis	did not bat			
S.D. Fletcher	did not bat			
Extras (b 1 lb 4 w 4 nb 7)		16		
Total (55 overs)		**244 for 6**		

YORKSHIRE	O	M	R	W	NORTHAMPTONSHIRE	O	M	R	W
Jarvis	11	2	43	4	Davis	11	1	37	0
Sidebottom	11	1	40	0	Walker	11	0	62	0
Fletcher	11	1	60	1	Capel	11	0	66	0
Hartley	11	0	66	2	N. Cook	11	1	42	1
Carrick	11	2	30	0	Williams	11	0	32	3

Umpires H.D. Bird and K.E. Palmer

1988

DERBYSHIRE v HAMPSHIRE

The 1988 Benson and Hedges Cup Final was a total disaster for Derbyshire. Even taking into account all the factors, the main one being the toss, Derbyshire did not play well enough. Hampshire, especially Steve Jefferies, dominated the match and Derbyshire could not even prolong it until tea.

Mark Nicholas, leading Hampshire into their first one-day final, lifted the trophy and there was never any other possible outcome once Derbyshire were dismissed for a paltry 117. It was the lowest total in a Benson and Hedges Final, taking over from Nottinghamshire's 130 against Somerset in 1982, and the lowest in any Lord's final. That unwanted distinction had previously belonged to Lancashire who were all out for 118 in the 1974 Gillette Cup Final against Kent.

Derbyshire, put in after Mark Nicholas had won the toss, failed with the bat. They were ripped apart by Steve Jefferies, pegged down by Nigel Cowley and finally committed suicide.

The start was certainly beguiling. Kim Barnett, Peter Bowler and extras had 25 on the board after only five overs. Barnett leaned out to drive Jefferies through extra cover and Bowler eased Cardigan Connor for four down the hill, cover-driving behind square. Even then the ball was zooming around, and if the Hampshire bowlers could begin to pitch it on the right spot there was trouble ahead!

Indeed, it was just around the corner. Barnett, already put down by Chris Smith at first slip off Connor, tried to drive Jefferies and edged the ball off his pads and into his stumps. That was the last ball of Jefferies' third over. For the first ball of the next, Nicholas summoned a helmet and stationed himself at short square-leg. Bowler obliged with an edge against his pads and walked without even looking at umpire David Constant. Steve Jefferies was now on a hat-trick and would have had it if Chris Smith had clung to a low edge from John Morris. In the same over, Bruce Roberts played the ball straight to Nicholas and when Steve Goldsmith was leg-before in Jefferies' next over, Derbyshire were in ruins at 32 for 4. Steve Jefferies had produced a great spell of swing bowling, taking four for one run over the space of eight balls.

Everything now depended on John Morris, the one major batsman left. Ideally, he and Bernie Maher had to see Derbyshire through to lunch, forget the scoring rate and keep some wickets in hand for the last 20 overs.

The batsmen worked hard. Morris was beaten by what was effectively a fast leg-break from Steve Andrew, and Maher survived a chance to Paul Terry at second slip. Inevitably it was slow going, although Morris straight drove Andrew and pulled Cardigan Connor for two fours.

They had added 39 in 17 overs when Maher tried to pull Jon Ayling and was bowled. It was a poor shot in the situation, so was Michael Holding's attempt to take on the spin of Nigel Cowley. Holding's big drive went straight to David Turner in front of the pavilion and because of a slight shower, it turned out to be the last ball before lunch.

Derbyshire's third self-inflicted disaster came after the county had reached 100 in the 37th over. John Morris turned Andrew to long-leg and charged back for a second run as Cowley was picking the ball up. Cowley's throw was good enough and Morris was run out for 42. It was a made second run and Morris knew it. Warner was then bowled by Jefferies and Connor returned with three wides. Then he adjusted his sights and bowled Paul Newman and Devon Malcolm with successive balls to complete the rout.

Derbyshire's only hope was for an early Hampshire collapse. Starting with a one-day field of four slips and a gully, Malcolm moved the ball away from Terry and Roberts held the catch at second slip. Chris Smith hit two fours off Newman and Nicholas eased Ole Mortensen to the square-leg boundary. Derbyshire picked up a second wicket when Chris Smith edged Mortensen to wicket-keeper Maher but then brother Robin began to hit the ball ferociously. Holding, who looked as if his hamstring had tweaked again, was dispatched through the covers as Robin Smith hit seven fours – as many as in the entire Derbyshire innings!

When Robin Smith, whose 38 off only 27 balls had given Hampshire both hands on the trophy, hooked at Alan Warner, the immediate reaction was that the top edge would land safely. Steve Goldsmith had other ideas – setting off from long-leg, he ran 40 yards while the ball was in the air, dived, completed the catch and came up triumphantly with the ball – one of the most brilliant outfield catches ever seen.

Derbyshire's misery was complete when a no-ball by Alan Warner provided Hampshire with their 118th and winning run.

John Morris

Devon Malcolm

GOLD AWARD WINNER 1988
STEVE JEFFERIES

Steve Jefferies had a long fight to establish himself in county cricket after beginning his career with Western province in his native South Africa.

He was looking for a place in 1982 and went on trial to Derbyshire. He played in one match against the Pakistan tourists at Chesterfield, but at the time John Wright and Peter Kirsten were Derbyshire's overseas

players. Jefferies went to Lancashire, and in three seasons took 87 wickets at an average of 29.51 and had a best of 8 for 46 against Nottinghamshire at Trent Bridge.

Released at the end of the summer of 1985, he returned to South Africa to concentrate on his career with Western Province. In the match against Orange Free State in 1987–88, he took all ten wickets in an innings for 59 runs – but despite this, he couldn't persuade Sussex to take him on.

In 1988, Hampshire, knowing that Gordon Greenidge and Malcolm Marshall would be with the West Indies team, engaged Australian paceman Bruce Reid. But Reid pulled out because of injury and they signed Jefferies who had spent the last two summers playing league cricket.

His early season performances were impressive and in the match against Gloucestershire he took 8 for 97. Yet Steve Jefferies will always be remembered by Hampshire followers for his 5 for 13 which significantly helped the county win their first Lord's final later that summer. His 18 wickets in the Benson and Hedges season of 1988 was a Hampshire record. It was without doubt the highlight of his two seasons with Hampshire and, although his left-arm swing bowling was less effective the following season, the decision to award him his county cap was popularly acclaimed.

A talented all-rounder, who never quite hit it off in England, Steve Jefferies played representative cricket for South Africa for a good number of years.

BENSON AND HEDGES CUP FINAL 1988

Played at Lord's, 9 July
Toss: Hampshire
Result: Hampshire won by seven wickets
Gold Award: Steve Jefferies
Adjudicator: Clive Lloyd

DERBYSHIRE

				Fall of Wickets	
K.J. Barnett	b Jefferies	13		1st	27
P.D. Bowler	c Nicholas b Jefferies	4		2nd	28
B. Roberts	c Nicholas b Jefferies	0		3rd	29
J.E. Morris	run out	42		4th	32
S.C. Goldsmith	lbw b Jefferies	0		5th	71
B.J. Maher	b Ayling	8		6th	80
M.A. Holding	c Turner b Cowley	7		7th	101
P.G. Newman	b Connor	10		8th	114
A.E. Warner	b Jefferies	4		9th	117
O.H. Mortensen	not out	0		10th	117
D.E. Malcolm	b Connor	0			
Extras (lb 14 w 12 nb 3)		29			
Total (46.3 overs)		**117 all out**			

HAMPSHIRE

				Fall of Wickets	
V.P. Terry	c Roberts b Malcolm	2		1st	10
C.L. Smith	c Maher b Mortensen	20		2nd	44
M.C.J. Nicholas	not out	35		3rd	90
R.A. Smith	c Goldsmith b Warner	38			
D.R. Turner	not out	7			
J.R. Ayling	did not bat				
S.T. Jefferies	did not bat				
R.J. Parks	did not bat				
N.G. Cowley	did not bat				
C.A. Connor	did not bat				
S.J.W. Andrew	did not bat				
Extras (lb 8 w 3 nb 5)		16			
Total (31.5 overs)		**118 for 3**			

HAMPSHIRE	O	M	R	W		DERBYSHIRE	O	M	R	W
Connor	7.3	1	27	2		Holding	11	2	36	0
Jefferies	10	3	13	5		Malcolm	7	2	25	1
Andrew	9	0	25	0		Newman	3	1	11	0
Ayling	9	2	21	1		Mortensen	5	1	19	1
Cowley	11	2	17	1		Warner	5.5	0	19	1

Umpires D.J. Constant and N.T. Plews

1989

ESSEX v NOTTINGHAMSHIRE

The sight of Nottinghamshire wicket-keeper Bruce French grabbing Eddie Hemmings and the pair doing an ecstatic victory jig on the Lord's pitch will be indelibly inscribed on the hearts of all who watched this amazing final.

Four runs to win off the last ball before a hushed full house – it was *Boy's Own* stuff! However, the central figures certainly were not in the full flush of youth themselves. Hemmings and John Lever were 40, having been born within four days of each other in February 1949. The tension as the Essex paceman prepared to bowl the final ball was made no less bearable by the deliberations with captain Graham Gooch about which field to set. Finally, they opted for a packed leg-side and it seemed that the only gap was either in front of or backwards of square on the offside.

Lever charged in off the sort of run which makes no concessions to age and the ball was a yorker on the off-stump. Hemmings got bat firmly on ball, though it took a veritable age before it hit the rope backward of square. Indeed, outfielder Brian Hardie was extremely close to getting a hand or foot to the ball as he chased desperately from the cover boundary.

This was Nottinghamshire's first Benson and Hedges Cup Final success. They had been hit by injury and were mauled by Somerset in the 1982 Final. And it was revenge for the 1985 NatWest defeat by Essex when everything also hinged on the last ball.

There was little hint seven hours earlier of the intense drama to come after Essex had won the toss and decided to bat in glorious sunshine. They lost Brian Hardie in only the third over, bowled by West Indian Franklyn Stephenson proving that nobody had a better slower ball.

It reduced Essex to 17 for 1, but with Gooch in imperious form and Alan Lilley playing the anchor role to perfection, it was a complete surprise when their stand of 70 in 17 overs ended. Left-armer Andy Afford, amply justifying his selection as a second spinner, got a ball to turn considerably and hit off-stump as Gooch tried a big hit to leg. Mark Waugh came in and played his shots from the off in another flourishing partnership of 92 with Lilley. But Nottinghamshire gave themselves a boost by dispatching Waugh in the last over before lunch at 156. Evans returned because Afford had completed his stint and had the Australian hitting straight into the hands of Tim Robinson at mid-wicket.

It was 152 for 4 in the 40th over when Paul Prichard fell leg-before to Cooper. Then John Stephenson sacrificed his wicket in an easy run-out so that Lilley might continue to progress. Lilley, whose innings was essentially intelligent though he showed his capacity to hit the ball hard, ultimately needed a six off Franklyn Stephenson's final delivery to reach his century. It simply brought a leg-bye towards the 32 extras which helped Essex to 243 for 7.

Though the total was short of Gooch's expectations, it still presented Nottinghamshire with the task of equalling the record score by a side batting second and winning the final.

They started disastrously, for only five runs had been scored in seven overs when Paul Pollard lost patience and hit across the line against Lever. At 17, Broad played an indiscriminate shot

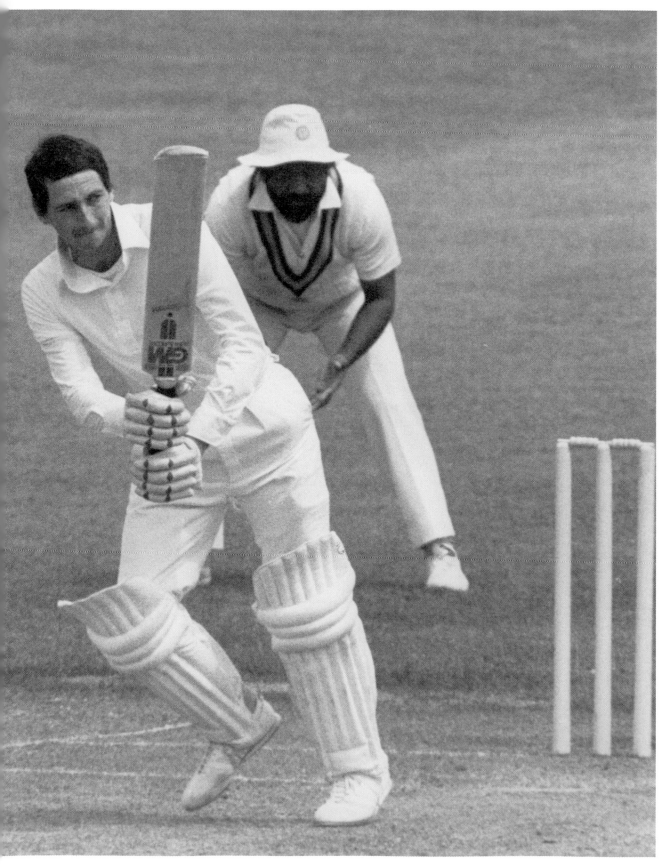

rek Randall

Mark Waugh

outside off-stump against the same bowler and was brilliantly caught by wicket-keeper Mike Garnham. But then Robinson, playing beautifully on both sides of the wicket, and Johnson steeled themselves not to surrender before tea.

After the interval, they accelerated brilliantly, adding 132 in 29 overs. They were separated at 149 when Johnson fell in bizarre fashion to Neil Foster, jumping over a straight ball which hit the wicket off his back leg. With the score on 162, Nottinghamshire's hopes were dealt a severe blow as Robinson responded to Randall's call and was run out for 86. But, though losing Stephenson first ball, Randall commendably shrugged off his inner turmoil to take over the main responsibility.

With ten still needed off seven balls, however, he perished going for a big leg-side hit. Nine was the target in the last over, entrusted to John Lever who had proved unusually expensive.

And Hemmings and French, two experienced cricketers, kept their nerve magnificently to add another trophy to that gained by the county two years earlier in the NatWest.

Nottinghamshire had any amount of individuals to thank for their success but Tim Robinson played a superb captain's innings – oozing responsibility and class – to deservedly win Ted Dexter's 'Man of the Match' award.

GOLD AWARD WINNER 1989
TIM ROBINSON

A great servant of Nottinghamshire County Cricket Club, Tim Robinson was a patient and watchful batsman who possessed the pleasant habit of dispatching off-line balls to the boundary.

He exceeded 1,000 runs in a season 14 times with a best of 2,032 in 1984. At the end of that season, he was selected to go on England's tour of India. After being unlucky to have been given out in each innings of his maiden Test in Bombay, he hit a faultless 160 in his second at Delhi, as England won by eight wickets. The following year, Robinson scored 175 against Australia at Headingley – only Worcestershire's R.E. Foster has made a higher score in his first Test against Australia. Not surprisingly he was voted as one of *Wisden*'s five 'Cricketers of the Year'.

Though he was ruthlessly exploited by the West Indian pace attack during England's 1985–86 tour of the Caribbean, he bounced back in 1987, hitting his fourth Test century, 166 against Pakistan at Old Trafford. During England's tour of New Zealand in 1987–88, Robinson demonstrated his ability to take the opposing attack apart with an innings of 166 against the Northern Districts at Hamilton – an innings that contained 10 sixes!

Tim Robinson's last Test appearance came against Sri Lanka in 1988, the year he was appointed captain of Nottinghamshire. He had appeared in twenty-nine Tests, scoring 1,601 runs at an average of 36.38.

Robinson captained the county until 1995, leading them to success in the Benson and Hedges Cup in 1989 and the Sunday League in 1991. He continued to represent Nottinghamshire until 1999, taking his total of first-class runs to 27,521 at an average of 42.15 and a highest score of 220 not out against Yorkshire at Trent Bridge in 1990.

BENSON AND HEDGES CUP FINAL 1989
Played at Lords, 15 July
Toss: Essex
Result: Nottinghamshire won by three wickets
Gold Award: Tim Robinson
Adjudicator: Ted Dexter

ESSEX

			Fall of Wickets	
G.A. Gooch	b Afford	48	1st	4
B.R. Hardie	b Stephenson	0	2nd	74
A.W. Lilley	not out	95	3rd	156
M.E. Waugh	c Robinson b Evans	41	4th	162
P.J. Prichard	lbw b Cooper	1	5th	185
J.P. Stephenson	run out	9	6th	220
D.R. Pringle	run out	15	7th	235
M.A. Garnham	c Johnson b Evans	0		
N.A. Foster	not out	2		
G. Miller	did not bat			
J.K. Lever	did not bat			
Extras (b 1 lb 26 w 4 nb 1)		32		
Total (55 overs)		**243 for 7**		

NOTTINGHAMSHIRE

			Fall of Wickets	
B.C. Broad	c Garnham b Lever	6	1st	5
P. Pollard	lbw b Lever	2	2nd	17
R.T. Robinson	run out	86	3rd	149
P. Johnson	b Foster	54	4th	162
D.W. Randall	c Waugh b Pringle	49	5th	162
F.D. Stephenson	c Gooch b Miller	0	6th	221
K.P. Evans	run out	26	7th	234
B.N. French	not out	8		
E.T. Hemmings	not out	6		
K.E. Cooper	did not bat			
J.A. Afford	did not bat			
Extras (b 1 lb 3 w 2 nb 1)		7		
Total (55 overs)		**244 for 7**		

NOTTINGHAMSHIRE	O	M	R	W		ESSEX	O	M	R	W
Stephenson	11	0	61	1		Lever	11	2	43	2
Cooper	11	3	30	1		Foster	11	1	40	1
Evans	11	0	28	2		Gooch	11	0	57	0
Afford	11	0	50	1		Pringle	11	1	38	1
Hemmings	11	0	47	0		Miller	9	0	50	1
						Stephenson	2	0	12	0

Umpires K.E. Palmer and D.R. Shepherd

1990

LANCASHIRE v WORCESTERSHIRE

Lancashire's all-round depth of talent proved too strong for Worcestershire. It was very much a case of David Hughes' men playing their aces at the right time throughout this eagerly awaited contest, and it was apparent well before the formal close that Worcestershire's woeful record of five defeats in five one-day final appearances was going to be extended to six out of six!

On a perfect summer's day, hot, sunny and cloudless, Worcestershire's captain Phil Neale won the toss and invited Lancashire to bat. England Test stars Fowler and Allott had shrugged off pre-match worries to allow Lancashire to field their strongest team, while Worcestershire brought back Neal Radford, who had been out for six weeks following abdominal surgery, for the unfortunate Graham Dilley, whose chronic knee was soon to go under the surgeon's knife!

In perfect batting conditions, Graeme Fowler and Gehan Mendis began brightly against the new ball attack of Newport and Botham. Fowler whipped the ball away for two leg-side fours in the second over but his mistimed drive off Newport in the seventh over was brilliantly caught by Neale at short mid-wicket, and in the next over Mendis was lucky to survive when D'Oliveira dropped him at first slip off Botham. The frustrated all-rounder immediately dropped him a short one and induced a skied mis-hook to the safe hands of Neale.

Mike Atherton

Ian Botham

Neil Fairbrother then joined Atherton, and with Botham and Newport taken out of the attack the left-hander unrolled two superb cover drives off Radford. But then, like his two predecessors, impatience got the better of him as he attempted an unwise pull off Lampitt and bottom-edged the ball on to his stumps.

Lancashire looked in trouble at 47 for 3 but Atherton and Watkinson embarked on a more than useful stand which saw the Red Rose county through to lunch at 119 for 3 off 37 overs. Atherton, who had taken on the role of anchorman, played one delightful late cut off Illingworth, while the more adventurous Watkinson plundered the bowling whenever possible.

However, shortly after play resumed, Lancashire suffered a double blow. First, Atherton was smartly run out by Lampitt's direct hit from mid-wicket. Then, with only a single added, Watkinson popped up a simple caught-and-bowled chance which Botham joyfully accepted.

It was after this that the two all-rounders, Wasim Akram and Phil DeFreitas, gave a much needed infusion of aggression to the innings. They smashed 55 off the next seven overs, their 50 partnership coming off 41 balls. In one memorable over off the bowling of Radford, Akram hit two huge sixes, one a short arm jab, the other a straight drive into the top deck of the pavilion. The Pakistani Test star had made 28 before Radford clung on to a catch off Newport and DeFreitas matched his score.

The final hectic overs were orchestrated by wicket-keeper Warren Hegg, who cut and carved his way to an unbeaten 31 off just 17 balls, hitting three fours and a big six off Botham. Ably supported by Austin, the last five overs produced 44 runs as the Lancashire score climbed to 241 for 8, leaving Worcestershire needing an overall run rate of 4.40 per over.

Curtis and Weston, who during the previous week had put on 188 against Somerset in the NatWest Trophy first round, began in circumspect fashion, but the introduction of Akram changed the course of the match. Akram replaced Phil DeFreitas at the Nursery End and his second ball was too quick for Curtis who could only fend it to Hegg. Graeme Hick was greeted by a vicious bouncer, deemed a no-ball. He looked visibly unsettled and four overs later with just one to his name, he fell to Akram in the same manner as Curtis. D'Oliveira, who was almost knocked over by a first ball yorker from Akram, lost his partner Weston in the next over, Watkinson finding a way between bat and pad. Two balls later, Botham, well forward, survived a confident leg-before shout.

Lancashire's bowling was tight, and at tea Worcestershire were 56 for 3 off 25 overs. Though the Worcestershire batsmen tried to increase the scoring rate after tea, the required rate kept climbing. D'Oliveira fell in the 31st over, missing a straight delivery from Watkinson. Neale, the last of the specialist batsmen, went without troubling the scorers, providing Warren Hegg with his third catch and Austin the first wicket of a tidy spell.

Botham called for his helmet when facing Akram but it was DeFreitas who ended Worcestershire's hopes when a fast, straight, short delivery kept low and trimmed Botham's off bail. His departure left Worcestershire at 114 for 7. The last dozen overs or so bore little resemblance to the usual one-day finale as Worcestershire slipped further behind the asking rate. The end came when Lampitt played on to Austin, leaving Lancashire as winners by 69 runs.

Adjudicator Bobby Simpson gave the Gold Award to Mike Watkinson although he might have been tempted to emulate Peter May in 1984 by voting for the Lancashire captain. Six years previously John Abrahams won the award for his leadership, even though he scored nought and didn't bowl. David Hughes didn't bowl either but probably spoiled his chances by scoring a single at the end of Lancashire's innings!

GOLD AWARD WINNER 1990
MIKE WATKINSON

It was Lancashire manager Jack Bond who plucked Mike Watkinson from the local leagues and threw him in at the deep end against Kent in August 1982. He earned his county cap the hard way, for when he was capped five years later he had already amassed 195 first team appearances.

Watkinson's willingness to bowl whenever, on whatever, and to whomever, made him a professional's professional.

Since Watkinson made his debut, Lancashire have actually had a good one-day side. Yet 'Winker' has often been the difference between the Red Rose side winning and nearly winning – a straight six to finish off the 1990 NatWest Final, a superb innings of 90 in the quarter-final win over Gloucestershire and match-winning performances with both seam and spin.

Watkinson performed the hat-trick against Warwickshire at Edgbaston in 1992 and a year later took 51 wickets and scored 1,016 runs – the first time for over thirty years that anyone had achieved that feat for the county. During the match against Hampshire at Old Trafford in 1994, he became only the third Lancashire player to score a century and take ten wickets in a match. The match also saw him produce his best ever bowling figures of 8 for 30.

Selected for England in 1995, his fitness and strength were testament to his dedication. If the selectors had chosen players for their workload, then Watkinson would have been capped much earlier. Even though he only appeared in four Tests against the West Indies, his innings of 82 not out at Trent Bridge saved England from defeat.

Appointed Lancashire captain in 1994, he led the side to Benson and Hedges Cup success in 1995 and 1996 and also to the NatWest Trophy in the latter year, when the county routed Essex. Now the county's senior coach, Watkinson's career figures of 10,564 runs at 26.67 and 711 wickets at 33.75 each do not flatter him and are not a true reflection of his worth.

BENSON AND HEDGES CUP FINAL 1990

Played at Lord's, 14 July
Toss: Worcestershire
Result: Lancashire won by 69 runs
Gold Award: Mike Watkinson
Adjudicator: Bobby Simpson

LANCASHIRE

				Fall of Wickets	
G.D. Mendis	c Neale b Botham	19		1st	25
G. Fowler	c Neale b Newport	11		2nd	33
M.A. Atherton	run out	40		3rd	47
N.H. Fairbrother	b Lampitt	11		4th	135
M. Watkinson	c and b Botham	50		5th	136
Wasim Akram	c Radford b Newport	28		6th	191
P.A.J. DeFreitas	b Lampitt	28		7th	199
I.D. Austin	run out	17		8th	231
W.K. Hegg	not out	31			
D.P. Hughes	not out	1			
P.J.W. Allott	did not bat				
Extras (lb 4 nb 1)		5			
Total (55 overs)	241 for 8				

WORCESTERSHIRE

				Fall of Wickets	
T.S. Curtis	c Hegg b Wasim Akram	16		1st	27
M.J. Weston	b Watkinson	19		2nd	38
G.A. Hick	c Hegg b Wasim Akram	1		3rd	41
D.B. D'Oliveira	b Watkinson	23		4th	82
I.T. Botham	b DeFreitas	38		5th	87
P.A. Neale	c Hegg b Austin	0		6th	112
S.J. Rhodes	lbw b Allott	5		7th	114
N.V. Radford	not out	26		8th	154
R.K. Illingworth	lbw b DeFreitas	16		9th	164
P.J. Newport	b Wasim Akram	3		10th	172
S.R. Lampitt	b Austin	4			
Extras (lb 9 w 8 nb 4)		21			
Total (54 overs)	**172 all out**				

WORCESTERSHIRE

	O	M	R	W
Newport	11	1	47	2
Botham	11	0	49	2
Lampitt	11	3	43	2
Radford	8	1	41	0
Illingworth	11	0	41	0
Hick	3	0	16	0

LANCASHIRE

	O	M	R	W
Allott	10	1	22	1
DeFreitas	11	2	30	2
Wasim Akram	11	0	30	3
Watkinson	11	0	37	2
Austin	11	1	44	2

Umpires J.H. Hampshire and N.T. Plews

1991

LANCASHIRE v WORCESTERSHIRE

This was an unusual match in a number of ways – the two teams involved were the same as in 1990; both teams had been knocked out of the NatWest Trophy the previous day; bad weather forced this one-day match into a second day, that day being, uniquely for a Lord's final, a Sunday; and finally Worcestershire won, putting an end to their miserable record of six defeats in six Lord's final appearances.

Lancashire's 44-year-old captain David Hughes decided to omit himself from the side for what would have been his tenth Lord's final.

It was a dull, overcast day and it was always going to be a struggle to finish the match on the first of the three days set aside after drizzle delayed the start by half-an-hour. Any hope of a one-day finish disappeared when Lancashire, having won the toss, dawdled through their overs slowly enough to receive four warnings from the umpires about the pace of their play.

If it had not been for Graeme Hick, most of the crowd would have departed on Saturday evening, completely disillusioned. Hick's Worcestershire captain Phil Neale had urged him to be positive after his recent poor form and Hick obeyed his captain's orders to the letter as he began by square-cutting his very first ball for four.

Hick had come in at the end of the opening over, when Tim Curtis chopped DeFreitas into his stumps. His determined display was in sharp contrast to Worcestershire's other star batsman, Australian Tom Moody, who struggled through 38 balls for just 12 before inside-edging Paul Allott into his stumps in the 12th over to leave them at a shaky 38 for 2.

It seemed a little strange that Hick was not confronted by Wasim Akram until the 16th over but by that time the Worcestershire batsman had worked out the vagaries of a rather bouncy Lord's wicket. Hick's third-wicket stand with Damien D'Oliveira ended shortly after lunch. They had added 59 in 14 overs when D'Oliveira spooned a catch to mid-off from a leading edge.

Enter Ian Botham to loud cheers – he proceeded to play second fiddle to Hick in a stand of 69 of which Beefy's share was a mere 16. Hick was just 12 short of a richly deserved century when he fell to an excellent one-handed return catch by the diving Paul Allott. Botham added just three before a massive pull off the bowling of Watkinson saw Fowler hang on to a well-judged catch in front of the Mound Stand.

Phil Neale sliced Austin to third man and Steve Rhodes and Phil Newport both skied Akram into safe hands. Worcestershire were 203 for 8 as Neal Radford joined Richard Illingworth. After a looping high no-ball, Radford lofted a well-timed six off his legs and smote two fours in a disappointing wayward last over from Akram. The over cost 18 and, with 10 more coming off Austin's last over of the innings, Worcestershire's final total was 236 for 8.

Graeme Fowler

Graham Dilley

Lancashire made a mixed start, with openers Fowler and Mendis both playing and missing against Dilley and then hitting him for well-struck boundaries. Lancashire's score had crept to 24 when Radford bowled Mendis through the gate. Shortly afterwards, Atherton, having been lucky to escape a leg-before appeal after playing no shot, touched a Radford lifter to the eager Rhodes.

Acting captain Neil Fairbrother pushed his second ball towards mid-wicket and ran but D'Oliveira hurtled in and threw down the stumps with the left-hander still short of his ground. At 32 for 3, the Lancashire players were grateful for the chance of an early tea, caused by the bad light, which shortly afterwards brought the day's entertainment to a close.

Sunday dawned considerably brighter, dry and sunny. Graham Lloyd, the extra batsman included in the Lancashire side at Hughes' expense, failed to add to his overnight total before being caught by Hick off a well pitched-up Botham delivery. Watkinson also fell to a thick slip catch, this time off the bowling of Dilley. Fowler had scored 54 when he edged the returning Radford to Hick, who took another good catch high to his left.

All-rounders Akram and DeFreitas represented the Red Rose county's last hopes but Rhodes ran out the Pakistani captain and a sharp catch by Neale at cover accounted for DeFreitas. Austin was the next to depart before Dilley persuaded Allott to heave almost vertically to cover where Worcestershire skipper Phil Neale again took the catch.

With 7.4 overs remaining and 65 runs to spare, Worcestershire had won their first one-day trophy at Lord's in an almost exact reversal of the previous year's result. Adjudicator Denis Compton, forced to shout after the Lord's PA system failed, gave the Gold Award to Graeme Hick.

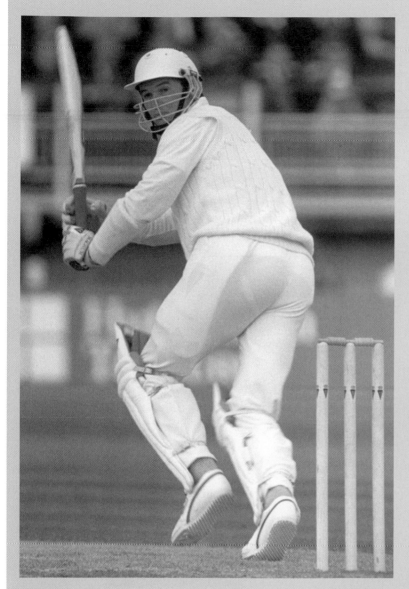

GOLD AWARD WINNER 1991 GRAEME HICK

The enigma of English cricket for the last decade, Graeme Hick made his Worcestershire debut in the final game of the 1984 season against Surrey at The Oval. The following summer he scored 1,265 first-class runs at an average of 52.70 and represented Zimbabwe on a short tour of England. He later decided to withdraw from the Zimbabwe side for the ICC Trophy to begin the long qualification for England.

The summer of 1986 was his first full season for Worcestershire, and, with successive scores of 227 not out against Nottinghamshire and 219 against Glamorgan, he became the first player to reach 1,000 runs. At the age of 20 he went on to become the youngest-ever player to score 2,000 runs in a season and was named as one of *Wisden*'s five 'Cricketers of the Year'.

In 1988 he produced one of the most amazing batting performances seen in English cricket when he scored 405 in the match against Somerset at Taunton. His overall aggregate for the season of 2,713 runs gave him an average of 77.51, effectively top of the national standings – his ten centuries equalled the Worcestershire record.

He finally qualified for England in 1991, and yet, though few players had come to the Test side with better credentials, it took him until his twenty-second Test before he scored his first hundred.

Over the years there have been doubts about Hick's ability to play real pace. Yet anyone who has seen Graeme Hick taking hundreds off Allan Donald, Franklyn Stephenson or Waqar Younis, or his magnificent innings against the West Indies at New Road in 1988, will tell you otherwise. There does seem to be a tendency in English cricket that when a player is super-talented – Hick has scored 35,055 first-class runs at 53.60 – any flaw in his game is magnified and exaggerated!

BENSON AND HEDGES CUP FINAL 1991

Played at Lord's, 13 and 14 July
Toss: Lancashire
Result: Worcestershire won by 65 runs
Gold Award: Graeme Hick
Adjudicator: Denis Compton

WORCESTERSHIRE

			Fall of Wickets	
T.S. Curtis	b DeFreitas	4	1st	4
T.M. Moody	b Allott	12	2nd	35
G.A. Hick	c and b Allott	88	3rd	97
D.B. D'Oliveira	c DeFreitas b Wasim Akram	25	4th	166
I.T. Botham	c Fowler b Watkinson	19	5th	172
P.A. Neale	c Watkinson b Austin	4	6th	175
S.J. Rhodes	c Allott b Wasim Akram	13	7th	195
R.K. Illingworth	not out	17	8th	203
P.J. Newport	c DeFreitas b Wasim Akram	2		
N.V. Radford	not out	25		
G.R. Dilley	did not bat			
Extras (lb 8 w 15 nb 4)		27		
Total (55 overs)		**236 for 8**		

LANCASHIRE

			Fall of Wickets	
G.D. Mendis	b Radford	14	1st	24
G. Fowler	c Hick b Radford	54	2nd	31
M.A. Atherton	c Rhodes b Radford	5	3rd	32
N.H. Fairbrother	run out	1	4th	64
G.D. Lloyd	c Hick b Botham	10	5th	92
M. Watkinson	c Hick b Dilley	13	6th	111
Wasim Akram	run out	14	7th	134
P.A.J. DeFreitas	c Neale b Newport	19	8th	140
W.K. Hegg	not out	13	9th	158
I.D. Austin	c Illingworth b Newport	7	10th	171
P.J.W. Allott	c Neale b Dilley	10		
Extras (lb 5 w 4 nb 2)		11		
Total (47.2 overs)		**171 all out**		

LANCASHIRE	O	M	R	W	WORCESTERSHIRE	O	M	R	W
DeFreitas	11	1	38	1	Dilley	8.2	2	19	2
Allott	11	3	26	2	Radford	9	1	48	3
Watkinson	11	0	54	1	Botham	8	1	23	1
Wasim Akram	11	1	58	3	Newport	11	1	38	2
Austin	11	0	52	1	Illingworth	11	0	38	0

Umpires J.W. Holder and D.R. Shepherd

1992
HAMPSHIRE v KENT

This was a meeting of two teams who had played each other only two days before in the NatWest Trophy, when Kent had been the victors. The only disappointment was that the climax of this match was watched by only around 8,000 spectators as the weather caused it to be carried over into the second day. There were some who said this outcome was in fact fortunate, as the weather forecast for the weekend made it likely that it could have been the first 'one-day' final to span three days!

Kent skipper Mark Benson won the toss and put Hampshire in to bat. While it was cloudy, there was nothing like the assistance bowlers in a NatWest Final would expect to get.

Terry and Middleton were one of the most reliable opening partnerships in the country, so it was something of a surprise when, in the 19th over, Middleton was adjudged leg-before to Carl Hooper for 27 with 68 on the board. Five overs later, Terry was bowled by the economical Igglesden, his innings of 41 including five fours.

This brought in David Gower to join Robin Smith and these two England Test stars forged the most productive partnership of the innings, adding 85 runs in 20 overs. Smith was in fine bludgeoning form, but Gower was far more restrained, scoring 25 singles in his 29, which came off 52 deliveries.

Conditions were certainly far from ideal for batting, with the light never better than moderate. There were two interruptions during the stand – one for lunch and a second, lasting 27 minutes, for rain.

The left-handed Gower eventually fell to Matthew Fleming, the second lbw victim of the innings and the first of two wickets to the irrepressible Old Etonian. But he was very expensive, conceding 63 runs in eight overs and Kent supporters wondered why left-arm spinner Richard Davis, whose five pre-lunch overs cost only 18, was not asked to bowl again in the innings.

Gower's dismissal brought Hampshire captain Mark Nicholas to the crease.

Paul Terry

Carl Hooper

Having missed the previous year's NatWest Final because of injury, he was anxious to do well and planted Fleming over the square-leg boundary for the first six of the day. He scored a brisk 25 before holing out to Ealham. Marshall then joined Smith, who had been content to play the minor role while Nicholas was in but who then hit the day's second six, also off Fleming over long-on.

Sadly, Smith was out 10 short of his century, run out responding to quite an unrealistic call by Marshall. The West Indian paceman made amends, hitting a four in each of the last two overs, and reaching 29 not out from 22 balls when the Hampshire innings ended at 253 for 5.

By now the light was dreadful, and it was quite a surprise that the Kent innings started. However, only eight deliveries were bowled before the umpires decided that the conditions were not good enough.

When play resumed on the Sunday morning, Trevor Ward played and missed several times before getting a touch to a magnificent Marshall delivery and providing Hampshire wicket-keeper Bobby Parks with the first of two catches. Jon Ayling then dismissed the dangerous

Neil Taylor, caught at the wicket chasing a wide one, and Kent were some way behind the asking rate with only 43 for 2 on the board after 20 overs.

Kent's main hope lay in Hampshire's less than brilliant ground-fielding, which was in complete contrast to the way the hop county had performed the previous day. Countless runs were saved by the Kent fielders, but Hampshire seemed to be wilting under the pressure with two boundaries coming in the 33rd over – both thanks to fielding errors.

Just in time, Hampshire pulled themselves together and two vital wickets fell just before lunch. Mark Benson was bowled by James – reward for a fine, accurate economical spell – and West Indian international Carl Hooper, the one man who could have swung things Kent's way, was bowled by Shaun Udal off his pads.

The afternoon session started with some bold blows by Fleming but he was brilliantly caught by Nicholas at mid-off. Kent's last five wickets fell for the addition of only 30 runs in the space of just four overs. Malcolm Marshall took two of them, Davis with the help of a stunning slip catch by Gower. Cardigan Connor bowled Mark Ealham, who had hit the only six of the Kent innings and grabbed two stumps – one for himself and one for Marshall.

With his unbeaten 29 at a vital stage of the Hampshire innings, and three wickets for only 33 runs, Malcolm Marshall would probably have been most people's choice for the Gold Award, but adjudicator Mickey Stewart gave it to Robin Smith, whose innings of 90 was by far the highest and best knock of the match.

GOLD AWARD WINNER 1992
ROBIN SMITH

A major force in Hampshire and England cricket, South African-born Robin Smith had produced a number of remarkable record-breaking feats in Natal and South African schools' cricket before joining his brother Chris at Hampshire.

A Championship debut hundred – 104 against Sussex at Basingstoke – followed by two more centuries in the space of ten innings in 1983 were ample proof of his class and temperament. Known as 'Judge' because of his wig-like hair, he qualified for England at the start of the 1985 season. Despite scoring freely over the next few seasons, including recording his maiden double century, 209 not out against Essex at Southend in 1987, it was the following summer before he made his Test debut.

By 1989, Robin Smith had emerged as England's number one middle-order batsman. His performances in the Ashes series won him a regular Test place as he hit two centuries in a total of 553 runs at an average of 61.44. Smith ended the summer top of England's Test and Hampshire's batting averages and was the highest placed English qualified player in the national averages. Despite a disappointing winter in Australia, he bounced back the following summer, scoring 416 runs against the West Indies at 83.20. Smith went on to play in sixty-two Tests for England, scoring 4,236 runs at 43.67, with a highest score of 175 against the West Indies at Antigua.

He was also a fine one-day player, having appeared in seventy-one limited-over games for England, scoring an unbeaten 167, an England record, against Australia at Edgbaston in 1993.

It is hard to believe that Robin Smith, who was appointed captain of Hampshire in 1998 and has scored 25,608 first-class runs at 41.70, last played Test cricket in the 1995–96 season.

BENSON AND HEDGES CUP FINAL 1992
Played at Lord's, 11 and 12 July
Toss: Kent
Result: Hampshire won by 41 runs
Gold Award: Robin Smith
Adjudicator: Mickey Stewart

HAMPSHIRE

			Fall of Wickets		
V.P. Terry	b Igglesden	41	1st	68
T.C. Middleton	lbw b Hooper	27	2nd	86
R.A. Smith	run out	90	3rd	171
D.I. Gower	lbw b Fleming	29	4th	205
M.C.J. Nicholas	c Ealham b Fleming	25	5th	234
M.D. Marshall	not out	29		
K.D. James	not out	2		
J.R. Ayling	did not bat			
R.J. Parks	did not bat			
S.D. Udal	did not bat			
C.A. Connor	did not bat			
Extras (lb 3 w 3 nb 4)		10		
Total (55 overs)		**253 for 5**		

KENT

			Fall of Wickets		
T.R. Ward	c Parks b Marshall	5	1st	17
M.R. Benson	b James	59	2nd	38
N.R. Taylor	c Parks b Ayling	8	3rd	116
C.L. Hooper	b Udal	28	4th	116
G.R. Cowdrey	c Gower b Marshall	27	5th	171
M.V. Fleming	c Nicholas b Ayling	32	6th	182
S.A. Marsh	b Udal	7	7th	186
M.A. Ealham	b Connor	23	8th	194
M.J. McCague	b Udal	0	9th	204
R.P. Davis	c Gower b Marshall	1	10th	212
A.P. Igglesden	not out	1		
Extras (b 1 lb 11 w 5 nb 4)		21		
Total (52.3 overs)		**212 all out**		

KENT	O	M	R	W	HAMPSHIRE	O	M	R	W
Igglesden	11	1	39	1	Connor	9.3	2	27	1
Ealham	9	0	46	0	Marshall	10	1	33	3
McCague	11	0	43	0	Ayling	11	0	38	2
Hooper	11	1	41	1	James	11	1	35	1
Davis	5	0	18	0	Udal	11	0	67	3
Fleming	8	0	63	2					

Umpires J.H. Hampshire and M.J. Kitchen

1993

DERBYSHIRE v LANCASHIRE

This was the year of the underdog. No one expected Derbyshire to win the Benson and Hedges Cup Final – beset by financial problems, they had to lay off three senior staff, while on the field they were without their overseas player, fast bowler Ian Bishop, who had suffered a long-term back injury. Yet they went to Lord's believing they were good enough to beat Lancashire, which they did after one of the most dramatic matches the famous ground has staged.

Put in to bat on a pitch of variable bounce, Derbyshire wobbled when Bowler was adjudged leg-before to DeFreitas in the first over. Derbyshire captain Kim Barnett was the next to go, dragging on a wide delivery from Wasim Akram, but it was an eventful second over from Mike Watkinson which threatened to destroy the batting side. John Morris flashed at a wide one and was caught behind, then Adams played on after surviving a confident lbw shout. In between, O'Gorman got off the mark with a five after DeFreitas's shy at the stumps from cover missed its target and raced to the boundary.

Chris Adams' brief innings was certainly one of the main talking points of the day. Two weeks before the final, in the Championship encounter between these two sides, which was settled by a last-day spell of 6 for 11 from Wasim Akram, Adams drew the umpire's attention (jokingly, he later claimed) to the state of the ball. The Pakistani captain's response at Lord's was to greet Adams, second ball, with a beamer – called a no-ball – which struck him on the shoulder. Unimpressed with the bowler's half-hearted apology – delivered with his back to the batsman while walking back to his mark – Adams confronted Akram over lunch, the pair reportedly having to be separated as they squared up to each other!

From a disappointing 66 for 4, Derbyshire were rescued by a sensible partnership from Cork and O'Gorman. Cork compiled his first one-day fifty, and by lunch the pair had doubled the score, Derbyshire 133 for 4. They took their stand to 109 before O'Gorman, one short of a deserved half century, touched one to Hegg. Griffith followed in identical fashion to his first ball, his departure coming 11 minutes after he took guard, thanks to an ill-timed shower of rain.

Cork and wicket-keeper Karl Krikken then added 77 in the final 11 overs. Cork finished with an unbeaten 92 and helped his side to 252 for 6, a total exceeded only twice by a side batting first in this showpiece final.

Needing a run rate of 4.6 to win, Lancashire got off to a flying start as Malcolm's first delivery to Atherton was a wide and the second was clipped for four. However, Warner's first over from the Nursery End saw Titchard well caught at second slip by Adams. Atherton went sedately on and he and Nick Speak advanced Lancashire's total to 78 for 1 off 25 overs at tea.

Speak fell for 42 shortly after the interval, bowled by Ole Mortensen, but Atherton and Fairbrother started to raise the tempo. Fairbrother flat-batted Malcolm through mid-on for four and Atherton hit successive boundaries off the bowling of Griffith. Lancashire had

Phil DeFreitas

reached 141 for 2 at the end of the 38th over, when heavy rain set in. The players trooped off and a Sunday finish – for the third year running – seemed a certainty. Then the rain stopped and the sun began to shine, and when the covers were removed play started again at 7.15.

Lancashire, it seemed, were in the driving seat, needing 112 to win off 17 overs with eight wickets in hand. Then Griffith held one back and gratefully clutched a return catch from Atherton who had just reached his half-century. Lloyd then fell lbw as he went down the track to Warner and the Derbyshire bowler soon struck a mortal blow when Akram chipped a catch back to him.

Neil Fairbrother then pulled Malcolm for six and narrowly failed to clear the pavilion rails with a sweetly timed straight hit off Frank Griffith. However, the required rate was rising to eight an over and beyond and although Phil DeFreitas flicked a Griffith full toss into the Mound Stand, Lancashire needed 11 off the final over. Frank Griffith had already conceded over 50 runs but he produced a superb over. DeFreitas heaved the third ball in the air for wicket-keeper Krikken to take the catch, and although Fairbrother then survived a run-out referral – third umpire John Holder having been unemployed throughout the rest of the game – the Lancashire skipper knew the game was up when he managed only a single off the penultimate ball. Lancashire ended up six runs short.

While one could feel sorry for Fairbrother, who finished unbeaten on 87, Derbyshire could always point to Dominic Cork, who in this match finally came of age on the big scene. Derbyshire's overdraft was reduced by the £30,000 prize money and captain Kim Barnett admitted: 'I had an inkling our name might be on the cup when we sneaked past Somerset in that quarter-final bowl-out at Taunton.'

Neil Fairbrother

GOLD AWARD WINNER 1993 DOMINIC CORK

Dominic Cork has hogged the cricket headlines during a controversial career that saw him take a wicket in his very first over for Derbyshire in their match against New Zealand in 1990. That summer, he played for Young England against Pakistan and in the third Test at Taunton, steered his side to safety with a battling innings of 110.

The following summer, he produced his best ever bowling figures for Derbyshire in their match against Essex at Derby. A muggy, overcast morning certainly favoured seam and swing bowling, and on what was his 20th birthday he took 8 for 53 before lunch!

Dominic Cork is blessed with a classically high action and a lively pace which allows him to bowl an awkward bouncer. He also possesses the ability to bowl a stock ball which, delivered close to the stumps, leaves the right-hander from middle and off.

Cork had made four England 'A' tours when he was finally rewarded with a Test debut against the West Indies at Lord's in 1995. After taking 7 for 43 he went on to perform the hat-trick in the fourth Test of that series at Old Trafford – the first by an England Test player for thirty years. Not surprisingly Cork's performances that summer were recognised by *Wisden* which made him one of its five 'Cricketers of the Year'.

Just when it seemed a glittering Test career beckoned, Cork missed England's winter tour of 1996–97 for personal reasons. He did, though, return to thrilling form against the West Indies in 2000, playing a crucial innings to steer his side to victory at Lord's.

Cork, who has played in thirty-four Tests, has now scored 6,629 first-class runs and taken 665 wickets – a ferocious competitor with an appetite for defying those who wrote him off!

BENSON AND HEDGES CUP FINAL 1993

Played at Lord's, 10 July
Toss: Lancashire
Result: Derbyshire won by 6 runs
Gold Award: Dominic Cork
Adjudicator: Cricket Writers' Club

DERBYSHIRE

			Fall of Wickets	
K.J. Barnett	b Wasim Akram	19	1st	7
P.D. Bowler	lbw b DeFreitas	4	2nd	32
J.E. Morris	c Hegg b Watkinson	22	3rd	61
C.J. Adams	b Watkinson	11	4th	66
T.J. O'Gorman	c Hegg b DeFreitas	49	5th	175
D.G. Cork	not out	92	6th	175
F.A. Griffith	c Hegg b DeFreitas	0		
K.M. Krikken	not out	37		
A.E. Warner	did not bat			
D.E. Malcolm	did not bat			
O.H. Mortensen	did not bat			
Extras (b 1 lb 11 w 1 nb 5)		18		
Total (55 overs)		**252 for 6**		

LANCASHIRE

			Fall of Wickets	
M.A. Atherton	c and b Griffith	54	1st	9
S.P. Titchard	c Adams b Warner	0	2nd	80
N.J. Speak	b Mortensen	42	3rd	150
N.H. Fairbrother	not out	87	4th	159
G.D. Lloyd	lbw b Warner	5	5th	184
Wasim Akram	c and b Warner	12	6th	218
M. Watkinson	b Cork	10	7th	243
P.A.J. DeFreitas	c Krikken b Griffith	16		
I.D. Austin	not out	0		
W.K. Hegg	did not bat			
A.A. Barnett	did not bat			
Extras (b 11 w 3 nb 6)		20		
Total (55 overs)		**246 for 7**		

LANCASHIRE	O	M	R	W		DERBYSHIRE	O	M	R	W
Austin	11	2	47	0		Malcolm	11	0	53	0
DeFreitas	11	2	39	3		Warner	11	1	31	3
Wasim Akram	11	0	65	1		Cork	11	1	50	1
Watkinson	11	2	44	2		Mortensen	11	0	41	1
Barnett	11	0	45	0		Griffith	11	0	60	2

Umpires B.J. Meyer and D.R. Shepherd

1994

WARWICKSHIRE v WORCESTERSHIRE

Warwickshire had become one of the hard-nosed positive teams in the country. Their six-wicket Benson and Hedges Cup Final win, completed with more than 10 overs to spare, was never the showpiece of their NatWest Trophy classic the previous September – but it meant that they had now completed an impressive limited-overs double in domestic cricket.

The final had been billed as the battle of the giants. Brian Lara had begun rewriting the record books with his innings of 375 against England in Antigua in April that year, following it with an astounding innings of 501 not out against Durham, against the likes of Graeme Hick and Tom Moody. But it was to be Paul Smith who stole the show! This would be another mightily impressive example of how Warwickshire, under the aggressive leadership of Dermot Reeve, had discovered the winning habit, justifying chief executive Dennis Amiss's belief that a golden age was dawning for the county.

From the moment Tim Munton bowled Adam Seymour at the start of the second over, Warwickshire's seam and swing bowlers kept the lid on a Worcestershire innings struggling to get any momentum. Gladstone Small and Munton produced a classic opening attack of movement through the air and off the pitch, but the former was hampered by a hamstring injury and bowled straight through his 11 overs. His success came in the 11th over when Tim Curtis, with the help of three boundaries, had made 13 of Worcestershire's 28. The former England paceman beat Curtis with an absolute beauty, drawing him to play outside off-stump to a ball which left him, found the edge and headed for the gloves of a diving Keith Piper.

That left Worcestershire looking to their big guns, Graeme Hick and Tom Moody, as they came together for a third-wicket partnership. But Moody was kept waiting 26 minutes for his first run as only six runs came from the next seven overs. If Worcestershire were hoping for some relief when Small and Munton finally took their sweaters, they received a nasty surprise. Paul Smith brought a delivery back sharply in his third over which defeated Hick and left Worcestershire at 55 for 3 in the 24th over. The England batsman had battled away for 90 minutes for 27 painstaking runs. Moody briefly loosened Warwickshire's grip by crashing Reeve over the top for his first boundary but runs were still at a premium as Worcestershire limped to 95 for 3 at lunch.

Wickets fell quickly after the restart with Neil Smith turning one sufficiently to find the edge of Gavin Haynes's bat. Paul Smith, who could bowl very quickly and hurry the best of batsmen, dismissed Leatherdale and Lampitt, while wicket-keeper Steve Rhodes went leg-before to Twose without troubling the scorers.

While Tom Moody remained at the crease, Worcestershire could still have posted a testing total. Though he was his side's top scorer with 47, he became so desperate that he got himself run out following Trevor Penney's brilliant piece of fielding from backward point. There followed a few lusty blows from Illingworth and Radford before Worcestershire's innings ended on 170 for 9.

Brian Lara

There was still enough juice in the pitch for Worcestershire to at least inflict similar damage in the early phase of Warwickshire's innings, but Tom Moody, Phil Newport and Stuart Lampitt failed to hit the right spots in line and length that might have curbed Warwickshire's reply.

As it was, the game was over as soon as Dominic Ostler and Roger Twose had seen off the new ball with some punishing stroke-play. The opening pair had put on 91 in quite serene style when their partnership was ended by a poor piece of cricket. Twose turned down a quick single and left Ostler stranded. He then failed to beat Gavin Haynes's throw from mid-on and ran himself out. There was a further flutter when Lara chipped Phil Newport to mid-wicket with the score at 103 but Paul Smith dismissed any thoughts of a history-making throwaway, stamping his authority on the game with a straight bat. Asif Din sensibly played second fiddle before being caught behind driving at Tom Moody.

It was fitting that 'Man of the Match' Paul Smith finished unbeaten on 42 alongside his captain Dermot Reeve, for it was he who instilled a terrific self-belief in the Warwickshire camp.

All this and not a mention of Lara – the West Indian world record holder hardly touched the ball in the field and made only eight with the bat as Warwickshire laid to rest the myth that they were a little more than a one-man team!

GOLD AWARD WINNER 1994
PAUL SMITH

The son and brother of county cricketers, Paul Smith was a vigorous all-rounder who played his first game for Warwickshire in 1982 at the age of 18. Capped four years later when he scored 1,508 runs at an average of 37.70, it was 1990 before he started to justify the faith people had in his ability. He had already performed the hat-trick against Northamptonshire at the County Ground in 1989 and repeated the achievement a year later against Sussex at Eastbourne. His change in fortune came from the confidence which resulted from both his own improved performances and those of his county. But then a cruel succession of injuries denied him. First it was his knee, then an Achilles tendon, and finally a broken finger.

Probably his biggest break came courtesy of Bob Woolmer, director of coaching at Edgbaston. Woolmer used his many South African contacts to obtain Smith a winter job with a Coloured club in Cape Town. He came back fully refreshed, and though there were those who considered him a bits and pieces player in county cricket, he proved very effective in limited-overs matches.

Useful to have around, he was capable of both quick runs – scoring an unbeaten 93 against Middlesex in the 1989 Sunday League – and a devastating burst of pace to get wickets – his best, 5 for 36, coming in the same competition against Worcestershire in 1993.

Paul Smith played the last of 221 games for Warwickshire in 1996, having scored 8,173 runs at 26.44 with a best of 140 against Worcestershire at New Road in 1989, and taken 283 wickets at 35.72 and a best bowling analysis of 6 for 91 against Derbyshire at Edgbaston in 1992.

BENSON AND HEDGES CUP FINAL 1994

Played at Lord's, 9 July
Toss: Warwickshire
Result: Warwickshire won by six wickets
Gold Award: Paul Smith
Adjudicator: Cricket Writers' Club

WORCESTERSHIRE

			Fall of Wickets	
T.S. Curtis	c Piper b Small	13	1st	10
A.C.H. Seymour	b Munton	3	2nd	28
G.A. Hick	lbw b P. Smith	27	3rd	55
T.M. Moody	run out	47	4th	100
G.R. Haynes	c Piper b N. Smith	22	5th	124
D.A. Leatherdale	c Ostler b P. Smith	4	6th	124
S.J. Rhodes	lbw b Twose	0	7th	125
S.R. Lampitt	c Penney b P. Smith	1	8th	126
R.K. Illingworth	lbw b Reeve	18	9th	168
N.V. Radford	not out	23		
P.J. Newport	not out	1		
Extras (lb 2 w 5 nb 4)		11		
Total (55 overs)		**170 for 9**		

WARWICKSHIRE

			Fall of Wickets	
D.P. Ostler	run out	55	1st	91
R.G. Twose	run out	37	2nd	98
B.C. Lara	c Hick b Newport	8	3rd	103
P.A. Smith	not out	42	4th	147
Asif Din	c Rhodes b Moody	15		
D.A. Reeve	not out	9		
T.L. Penney	did not bat			
K.J. Piper	did not bat			
N.M.K. Smith	did not bat			
G.C. Small	did not bat			
T.A. Munton	did not bat			
Extras (lb 1 w5)		6		
Total (44.2 overs)		**172 for 4**		

WARWICKSHIRE

	O	M	R	W
Small	11	4	26	1
Munton	11	3	29	1
P. Smith	11	1	34	3
Reeve	9	1	38	1
N. Smith	5	0	16	1
Twose	8	1	25	1

WORCESTERSHIRE

	O	M	R	W
Moody	11	2	31	1
Newport	8	0	29	1
Lampitt	9.2	1	38	0
Illingworth	6	0	22	0
Radford	8	0	39	0
Hick	2	0	12	0

Umpires H.D. Bird and K.E. Palmer

1995
KENT v LANCASHIRE

This is the only Benson and Hedges Cup Final when the Gold Award went to a member of the losing side. Kent's Aravinda de Silva made 112 off 95 balls, yet Lancashire lifted the Cup and his magnificent effort was in vain.

Kent were being tormented by the accuracy of Ian Austin when Aravinda opened his account with two pulled sixes into the Mound Stand. While no other Kent batsman could muster more than 25, he went to his hundred with another pulled six and a scintillating off-drive. So much for the nervous 90s! When he was finally caught on that peppered Mound Stand boundary, he bashed his pads in anguish while all Lancashire rejoiced with great relief. He could have won the match on his own. Not surprisingly, he was accorded a standing ovation all the way from the crease.

Lancashire's semi-final match against Worcestershire saw Graeme Hick score 116, his third Benson and Hedges century of the summer as his side totalled 261. In reply Lancashire struggled to 169 for 7 with just 11 overs to go. Then Wasim Akram hit an amazing 64 off 47 balls to secure a most unlikely last-over victory for the Red Rose county.

Kent had suffered a serious setback in the run-up to the Final. Their captain and prolific batsman Mark Benson had a broken finger and so was out of the game. It was a series of five century opening partnerships between Benson and Trevor Ward that had taken Kent to Lord's. Benson's stand-in, wicket-keeper Steve Marsh, won the toss and asked Lancashire to bat.

In the very first over of the game, left-arm seamer Tim Wren found

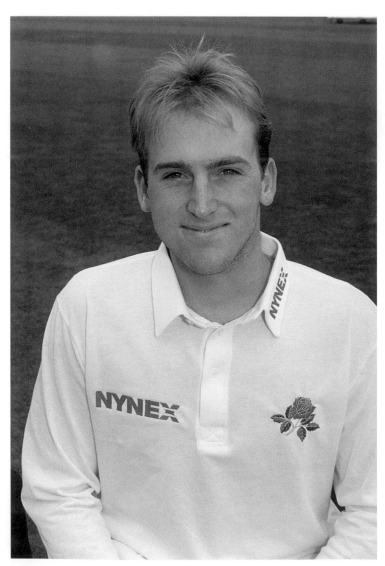

John Crawley

The victorious Lancashire team

the edge of Mike Atherton's bat, the ball falling just short of de Silva at fine leg. If it had gone to hand then the whole course of the game could have been completely different. Atherton and Gallian added 80 for the first wicket before Mark Ealham bowled the Australian-born opener for 36.

The more aggressive John Crawley joined Atherton, the two of them sharing a partnership of 121 for the second wicket, before the then England captain gave a catch in the deep off the bowling of Dean Headley when just seven runs short of his century. Neil Fairbrother also fell to Headley, before Crawley, who had pushed on, hitting Martin McCague for a huge six, was dismissed by the Kent bowler for 83. Graham Lloyd was then run out by McCague before the Kent paceman also helped to dismiss Wasim Akram in similar fashion. Though his 11 overs had been expensive, McCague had a hand in the final wicket to fall, catching Lancashire skipper Mike Watkinson off the bowling of Matthew Fleming. Lancashire's total of 274 for 7 off their 55 overs was the second highest score in the history of the Benson and Hedges Cup Finals.

As Kent's bowlers had struggled for direction, so their batsmen failed to build on partnerships. Trevor Ward's awesome run in the competition came to an end when he was caught behind by Hegg off the bowling of Glen Chapple. It wasn't a bad shot, it just bounced more than he expected. His opening partner David Fulton was next to go, leg-before to Chapple for 25. This brought to the wicket the 5 ft 2 in Sri Lankan batsman, Aravinda de Silva.

Lancashire off-spinner Gary Yates, who was always searching for ways of creating pressure or taking a wicket, took the next three, dismissing Taylor, Cowdrey and Fleming to leave Kent on 162 for 5.

While de Silva was playing so confidently he could win the game almost single-handedly, but partnerships did not develop and, following Ealham's dismissal, the Sri Lankan was kept off strike at crucial times. He was eventually out with the score on 214, caught in the deep by Graham Lloyd, who not surprisingly was mobbed by his delighted team-mates. The successful bowler was Ian Austin, who then removed Kent's acting captain Steve Marsh before Watkinson ended the match with the wickets of Headley and Wren.

Thus Lancashire collected the trophy and did so deservedly, looking as good as any post-war Red Rose side.

GOLD AWARD WINNER 1995
ARAVINDA DE SILVA

Aravinda de Silva's father Sam ensured that he took up cricket. His mother Indrani wanted him to play tennis because it used up less study time! Batting became his preoccupation from the age of nine, thanks to a succession of coaches – Charlie Warnakulasuriya, Wan Silva, Walter Perara and Ranjith Fernando.

He first came over to England to watch the World Cup as Schoolboy Cricketer of the Year in 1979 but returned five years later when he made his Test debut for Sri Lanka at Lord's. He also captained his country there against England in 1991. In only his second Test against India in Colombo in 1985–86, Sri Lanka needed to score 123 off 11 overs to record their first win in Tests. Aravinda, who usually batted at No. 7 or 8, was promoted to open. He hit Kapil Dev for six off the first ball of the innings and Dev's opening over accrued 17 runs. But the chase was called off when three wickets fell in eight balls. He is perhaps the only player in Test history to have reached the century landmark by hitting a six on three occasions, including his maiden hundred! That says something about his attitude towards batting, which transcends the pressures of the Test arena.

With Carl Hooper likely to be touring with the West Indies, Kent began discussions with de Silva for him to become their overseas player for 1995. It did not take him long to decide! Adjusting his play to suit the extra movement in English conditions, playing much straighter than usual, it was not long before he became the first player to reach 1,000 Championship runs. In one month he scored 779 runs in the Championship alone at an average of 129.80 including two double centuries, followed by his marvellous century in the Benson and Hedges Final. As if that were not enough he scored a century against the West Indies five days later, with Kent following on after being dismissed for 95 in just 18.4 overs.

Aravinda has now played in eighty-nine Tests and only Arjuna Ranatunga has more Sri Lankan caps. He has scored 5,952 runs with 19 centuries at an average of 41.91 and he also has 275 one-day internationals to his name.

BENSON AND HEDGES CUP FINAL 1995

Played at Lord's, 15 July
Toss: Kent
Result: Lancashire won by 35 runs
Gold Award: Aravinda de Silva
Adjudicator: Cricket Writers' Club

LANCASHIRE

				Fall of Wickets	
M.A. Atherton	c Fulton b Headley	93		1st	80
J.E.R. Gallian	b Ealham	36		2nd	201
J.P. Crawley	c Taylor b McCague	83		3rd	236
N.H. Fairbrother	c McCague b Headley	16		4th	258
G.D. Lloyd	run out	12		5th	259
Wasim Akram	run out	10		6th	266
M. Watkinson	c McCague b Fleming	0		7th	274
I.D. Austin	not out	5			
W.K. Hegg	did not bat				
G. Chapple	did not bat				
G. Yates	did not bat				
Extras (lb 2 w 10 nb 7)		19			
Total (55 overs)		**274 for 7**			

KENT

				Fall of Wickets	
D.P. Fulton	lbw b Chapple	25		1st	28
T.R. Ward	c Hegg b Chapple	7		2nd	37
N.R. Taylor	b Yates	14		3rd	81
P.A. de Silva	c Lloyd b Austin	112		4th	142
G.R. Cowdrey	lbw b Yates	25		5th	162
M.V. Fleming	b Yates	11		6th	180
M.A. Ealham	lbw b Watkinson	3		7th	214
S.A. Marsh	c Crawley b Austin	4		8th	214
M.J. McCague	not out	11		9th	219
D.W. Headley	c Chapple b Watkinson	5		10th	239
T.N. Wren	c Austin b Watkinson	7			
Extras (lb 7 w 2 nb 6)		15			
Total (52.1 overs)		**239 all out**			

KENT	O	M	R	W	LANCASHIRE	O	M	R	W
Wren	5	0	21	0	Wasim Akram	10	0	57	0
Headley	11	0	57	2	Chapple	10	1	55	2
McCague	11	0	65	1	Austin	11	4	36	2
Ealham	11	0	33	1	Watkinson	10.1	0	42	3
de Silva	8	0	36	0	Yates	11	0	42	3
Fleming	9	0	60	1					

Umpires N.T. Plews and D.R. Shepherd

1996
LANCASHIRE v NORTHAMPTONSHIRE

Cup holders Lancashire were back at Lord's for their sixth appearance in a one-day final in seven seasons. Not only had they won the trophy the previous year, but they had won fourteen Benson and Hedges matches in a row to reach their second consecutive final. While Lancashire were without doubt clear favourites for this match, Northamptonshire had played in nine Lord's finals, but had lost six of them.

This was also the first Benson and Hedges Cup Final to be contested over 50 overs and the first to allow just two fielders in the deep for the first 15 overs of the match. Also, it was the first final with a mid-afternoon lunch!

This summer also saw the 'pinch-hitter' – a batsman who would open the innings and try and take advantage of the wide open spaces in the deep. Lancashire's pinch-hitter was their captain Mike Watkinson but he was the first wicket to fall when he hit Taylor into the hands of John Emburey. Jason Gallian was then run out by Tony Penberthy with the score on 52 to bring John Crawley to the wicket. He was in fine form and with four fluent boundaries looked set for a good score when he was caught by Warren off the bowling of Penberthy. Though Mike Atherton had been extremely patient in compiling his innings of 48, he was out with the score on 131, dismissed by the combination of Northants' new skipper Rob Bailey and the old campaigner, 43-year-old John Emburey, who had been brought to Wantage Road as the club's chief coach!

Graham Lloyd's innings of 26 at more than a run a ball threatened to put the game completely out of Northamptonshire's reach but Paul Taylor was recalled to the

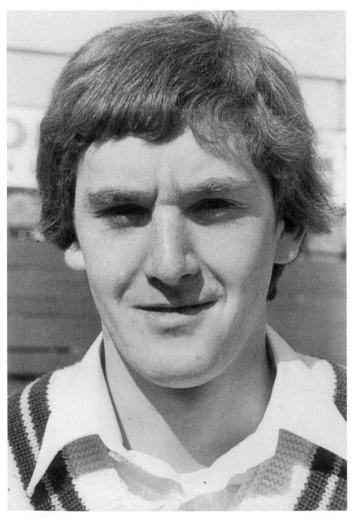

Rob Bailey

Glen Chapple

attack and responded by uprooting the Lancashire batsman's off-stump. Wicket-keeper Warren Hegg was run out before Neil Fairbrother, Lancashire's top scorer, was bowled by David Capel. The little left-hander had been his usual self, hitting six boundaries in a fine innings of 63 off just 70 balls. Yates failed to trouble the scorers before Curtly Ambrose caught and bowled Ian Austin, who scored 14 valuable runs at the death.

Ian Austin then had Capel caught behind with just one run on the board and after this saw Alan Fordham chop the ball onto his stumps with the score on 10. The burly Lancastrian went on to bowl his first seven overs for just seven runs!

A third-wicket partnership of 87 followed between Rob Bailey and Richard Montgomerie, before the Northamptonshire skipper provided Hegg with his second catch of the innings off the bowling of Chapple. Moments later, Montgomerie became Hegg's third victim when he got a thin inside-edge to a slower ball from off-spinner Gary Yates.

Lancashire captain Mike Watkinson then removed both Warren and Walton to leave Northamptonshire on 184 for 6. This quickly became 186 for 7 when Kevin Curran's fine knock came to an end.

With Northamptonshire now needing a Neil Fairbrother-type innings and eight runs an over from the ten that remained, Ian Austin returned to the attack. In the first of his final three overs, he bowled John Emburey, then saw Curtly Ambrose run out before demolishing the wickets of Tony Penberthy to give Lancashire a 31-run victory.

Austin's 4 for 21 from 9.3 overs ensured that the Red Rose county retained the trophy and won him the Gold Award. A true professional's professional, Austin was later called into the England one-day international team and followed this with another 'Man of the Match' award in the NatWest Trophy Final.

Lancashire's victory meant that they were the first county to win the Benson and Hedges Cup Final four times and the second after Somerset to win the trophy in successive years.

GOLD AWARD WINNER 1996 IAN AUSTIN

After some steady performances with both bat and ball in Championship and one-day games, Ian Austin was awarded his county cap in 1990. The following year in the Roses match at Scarborough, the Lancashire all-rounder hit what was not only his maiden first-class century, but also the season's fastest hundred in 68 minutes off 61 balls to win the Lawrence Trophy.

Austin's bowling was usually economical and in 1994 he produced match figures of 10 for 60 (5 for 23 and 5 for 37) in the match against Middlesex at Old Trafford.

In 1997, Austin and Graham Lloyd set a new county seventh-wicket record partnership of 248 in just 31 overs in the Roses match at Headingley; Austin's share was 83. Later that summer he scored a splendid 97 in the NatWest Trophy match against Sussex at Hove – this adventurous batting, coupled with his line and length bowling, won him selection for England in limited-overs competition. Sadly he failed to do himself justice.

There is no doubt that Austin's best season for Lancashire was 1997 when he scored 825 runs and captured 47 wickets. In 1998 he was named 'Man of the Match' in Lancashire's NatWest Trophy Final victory over Derbyshire with figures of 3 for 14 off his 10 overs.

Granted a benefit in 2000, 'Oscar' scored 3,778 runs at 27.98, with a highest score of 115 not out against Derbyshire at Blackpool in 1992, and took 262 wickets at 30.35 each with a best of 6 for 43 against Sri Lanka 'A' at Old Trafford in 1999 before parting company with the Red Rose county.

BENSON AND HEDGES CUP FINAL 1996

Played at Lord's, 13 July
Toss: Lancashire
Result: Lancashire won by 31 runs
Gold Award: Ian Austin
Adjudicator: Cricket Writers' Club

LANCASHIRE

			Fall of Wickets	
M.A. Atherton	c Bailey b Emburey	48	1st	18
M. Watkinson	c Emburey b Taylor	7	2nd	52
J.E.R. Gallian	run out	17	3rd	105
J.P. Crawley	c Warren b Penberthy	34	4th	131
N.H. Fairbrother	b Capel	63	5th	180
G.D. Lloyd	b Taylor	26	6th	203
W.K. Hegg	run out	11	7th	236
I.D. Austin	c and b Ambrose	14	8th	236
G. Yates	c Penberthy b Capel	0	9th	243
G. Chapple	not out	6		
P.J. Martin	not out	1		
Extras (w 10 nb 8)		18		
Total (50 overs)		**245 for 9**		

NORTHAMPTONSHIRE

			Fall of Wickets	
D.J. Capel	c Hegg b Austin	0	1st	1
A. Fordham	b Austin	4	2nd	10
R.J. Bailey	c Hegg b Chapple	46	3rd	97
R.R. Montgomerie	c Hegg b Yates	42	4th	111
K.M. Curran	c Crawley b Chapple	35	5th	132
R.J. Warren	c Crawley b Watkinson	11	6th	184
T.C. Walton	st Hegg b Watkinson	28	7th	186
A.L. Penberthy	b Austin	8	8th	194
J.E. Emburey	b Austin	6	9th	214
C.E.L. Ambrose	run out	10	10th	214
J.P. Taylor	not out	0		
Extras (lb 10 w 12 nb 2)		24		
Total (48.3 overs)		**214 all out**		

NORTHAMPTONSHIRE	O	M	R	W	LANCASHIRE	O	M	R	W
Ambrose	10	2	35	1	Austin	9.3	2	21	4
Taylor	9	0	55	2	Martin	9	2	32	0
Curran	7	0	48	0	Chapple	10	1	51	2
Capel	8	1	37	2	Watkinson	10	0	66	2
Penberthy	6	0	31	1	Yates	10	0	34	1
Emburey	10	1	39	1					

Umpires M.J. Kitchen and G. Sharp

1997
KENT v SURREY

The two finalists had emerged from the same zonal group, with the match between them at The Oval being won by the visitors Kent with a six off the last ball! And though Kent were at Lord's for their eighth Benson and Hedges Final, they had lost their last three and hadn't won at the home of cricket for nine years.

Surrey had reached the final with a quarter-final victory over Essex, whose top order had been completely blown away by Martin Bicknell and Chris Lewis, while in the semi-final, they had set opponents Leicestershire far too stiff a target.

Alec Stewart

Chris Lewis

Kent won the toss and elected to bat, but the day didn't start well for them. Surrey's strike force of Chris Lewis and Martin Bicknell reduced them to 23 for 3 in the seventh over as they bowled in the areas where it's difficult to hit. Walker lost his off-stump to Bicknell while both Fleming and Wells were adjudged leg-before. Nigel Llong proved to be a stumbling block, first adding 43 for the fourth wicket with Trevor Ward and then 38 for the fifth with Mark Ealham and though this provided some fight-back, Kent had only reached 106 in the 30th over when Llong fell to Saqlain Mushtaq for 42. Graham Cowdrey didn't last too long before he became Chris Lewis's second victim as he played on to the England all-rounder.

Kent's England all-rounder Mark Ealham was batting beautifully and along with the county's overseas player, Zimbabwean leg-spinner Paul Strang, added 35 for the seventh wicket before the latter was bowled by Salisbury for 23. Kent captain and wicket-keeper Steve Marsh joined Ealham and the two continued to put bat to ball until Ealham, who was his side's top scorer with 52 became another of Lewis's victims. McCague fell to Saqlain's third ball, having failed to trouble the scorers, leaving Marsh and Headley to take the Kent total to 212 for 9.

The Surrey innings got off to a disastrous start when their opening batsman, Alistair Brown, was caught in the gully by Matthew Fleming off the bowling of McCague with just two runs on the board. Nineteen-year-old Ben Hollioake came in to join Alec Stewart to play only his second innings at Lord's – the first having been a one-day international the previous May when he had made 63 on his international debut! That day, the young Hollioake had showed himself to be a big occasion player and proved in this Benson and Hedges Final that it wasn't just a flash in the pan.

Though he was nearly caught and run out off the same ball early on, he just timed the ball straight away. Over the next 33 overs, Hollioake and Stewart added 159 runs – with the young Hollioake's contribution being 98 from just 113 balls faced. Unfortunately he fell just two runs short of his hundred, caught at mid-on by Strang off the bowling of Mark Ealham. Not surprisingly, a rapturous reception greeted his return to the pavilion.

It was then left to Surrey's two elder statesmen, England stars Alec Stewart (75 not out) and Graham Thorpe (17 not out), to complete what by now had become the formality of an easy Surrey win by eight wickets and with five overs to spare.

Ben's brother, Adam Hollioake, who had replaced Alec Stewart as the county captain for the start of the 1997 season and who was the next batsman in, lifted the Benson and Hedges Cup.

Kent skipper Steve Marsh, who was captaining a Benson and Hedges losing team for the third time, was magnanimous in defeat, saying that Kent 'simply did not compete on the day'.

GOLD AWARD WINNER 1997
BEN HOLLIOAKE

The younger brother of Surrey captain Adam Hollioake, the Melbourne-born player was taken onto The Oval staff in 1995 and made his first-class debut the following year, aged just 18. He was a genuine all-rounder – the complete three-in-one player and therefore always in the game.

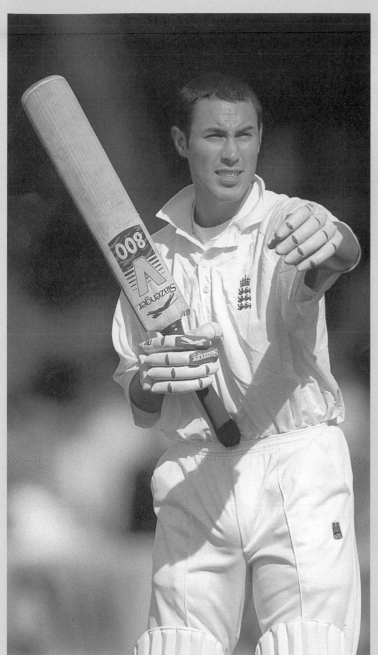

In 1997 he was hailed as England's new star and on his one-day international debut scored a superb 63 against Australia at Lord's. Shortly after his innings in the Benson and Hedges Cup Final, he made his Test debut alongside his brother Adam in the Trent Bridge Test. Though great things were expected of him, they were perhaps a little premature, for at that time he had yet to make a century or take more than four wickets in an innings in the first-class game.

Voted both the PCA and Cricket Writers' Club 'Young Cricketer of the Year' for 1997, Hollioake toured Sri Lanka with England 'A' where he made the highest score of his career, 163 against Sri Lanka 'A' at Moratuwa.

Timing was the feature to stand out in his batting – the way he got off the mark against Australia, back down the ground, saying it all. His highest score for Surrey was 118 against Yorkshire at The Oval in 2001, while on the bowling front, he was capable of being genuinely quick. His best figures for Surrey were 5 for 51 against Glamorgan in 1999.

Hollioake's fielding was quite breathtaking – he possessed it all: speed, anticipation, agility, good hands and a superb arm, not to mention reactions that at times defied belief.

The only player to win two Benson and Hedges Cup Final Gold Awards, he loved the game of cricket but it was not the be all and end all for him. Ben Hollioake wanted to live life to the full.

Sadly, Surrey lost the heartbeat of their side when on 23 March 2002, Ben Hollioake died in a car crash in Perth, Western Australia.

BENSON AND HEDGES CUP FINAL 1997
Played at Lord's, 12 July
Toss: Kent
Result: Surrey won by eight wickets
Gold Award: Ben Hollioake
Adjudicator: Cricket Writers' Club

KENT

			Fall of Wickets	
M.V. Fleming	lbw b Lewis	7	1st	15
M.J. Walker	b Bicknell	6	2nd	15
T.R. Ward	lbw b A. Hollioake	15	3rd	23
A.P. Wells	lbw b Bicknell	5	4th	68
N.J. Llong	c Butcher b Saqlain Mushtaq	42	5th	106
M.A. Ealham	c Brown b Lewis	52	6th	135
G.R. Cowdrey	b Lewis	8	7th	170
P.A. Strang	b Salisbury	23	8th	194
S.A. Marsh	not out	24	9th	198
M.J. McCague	c Thorpe b Saqlain Mushtaq	0		
D.W. Headley	not out	3		
Extras (b 1 lb 7 w 17 nb 2)		27		
Total (50 overs)		**212 for 9**		

SURREY

			Fall of Wickets	
A.D. Brown	c Fleming b McCague	2	1st	2
A.J. Stewart	not out	75	2nd	161
B.C. Hollioake	c Strang b Ealham	98		
G.P. Thorpe	not out	17		
A.J. Hollioake	did not bat			
M.A. Butcher	did not bat			
C.C. Lewis	did not bat			
J.D. Ratcliffe	did not bat			
M.P. Bicknell	did not bat			
I.D.K. Salisbury	did not bat			
Saqlain Mushtaq	did not bat			
Extras (lb 11 w 6 nb 6)		23		
Total (45 overs)		**215 for 2**		

SURREY	O	M	R	W	KENT	O	M	R	W
Bicknell	8	0	33	2	McCague	8	0	45	1
Lewis	10	3	39	3	Headley	10	0	53	0
A. Hollioake	7	0	31	1	Fleming	7	1	29	0
B. Hollioake	6	0	28	0	Ealham	6	0	31	1
Saqlain Mushtaq	9	1	33	2	Strang	10	1	31	0
Salisbury	10	0	40	1	Llong	4	0	15	0

Umpires G. Sharp and D.R. Shepherd

1998

ESSEX v LEICESTERSHIRE

Essex captain Paul Prichard had missed the whole of his team's Benson and Hedges Cup exploits while recovering from a stress fracture to his left leg, but he managed to recover just in time to lead from the front in the Final.

The weather forecast for the weekend of this Final was dire to say the least and looked likely to aid swing bowling. Leicestershire captain Chris Lewis – playing in a Benson and Hedges Final for the second year in a row, but for a different county – won the toss and put Essex in.

Despite the clouds building, the Leicestershire bowlers failed to make the best of the conditions, although there were occasions when Alan Mullally was able to bowl one or two completely unplayable deliveries. Prichard and Stuart Law both played and missed but took the score to 40 after 10 overs when the Australian was caught at mid-wicket by Mullally off the bowling of Vince Wells for six.

The incoming batsman was Nasser Hussain, who had led Essex through all the earlier stages of the competition. He and Prichard added 134 for the second wicket in 25 overs but when just eight runs short of a well-deserved century, the Essex skipper cut Dominic Williamson to backward point where Phil Simmons clung on to a good catch. Disappointed as he was not to reach three figures, the significance of his innings was not lost on an appreciative Lord's crowd.

Mark Ilott

Nasser Hussain

Hussain and new batsman Ronnie Irani then proceeded to hit a quickfire 60 before the England captain, whose use of the reverse sweep brought him a number of runs, fell to Chris Lewis for 88. Danny Law didn't last long before Alan Mullally returned towards the end of the Essex innings to pick up three wickets. Essex's total of 268 for 7 was quite a good one, but as the players walked off, the rain that had been threatening all day began to fall. It intensified during the interval, and after a short discussion it was agreed that Leicestershire would not be able to start their innings until the following day.

Early on Sunday morning, the rain was still falling and despite the comprehensive covering at Lord's, it didn't look as if any play would be possible. Umpires and captains agreed a cut-off time for the start and plans were also made for resolving the outcome with a bowl-out at a set of undefended stumps.

But the rain suddenly stopped and play got under way just before half-past three. Batting was obviously not going to be easy and Leicestershire openers Darren Maddy, who had already earned a one-day international call-up for England, and Iain Sutcliffe had reached only six in as many overs against the new ball bowling of Mark Ilott and Ashley Cowan. With no addition to the score, Cowan took two wickets, having Sutcliffe and new batsman Ben Smith caught at slip by Stuart Law. Maddy was joined by West Indian Test star Phil Simmons but Ilott's accuracy was eventually rewarded when he hit the top of Simmons' off-stump to leave Leicestershire 10 for 3.

Ilott then dismissed Wells in the ninth over and with just 15 overs gone, the Leicestershire batting was in tatters as both Cowan and Ilott picked up another wicket apiece. Aftab Habib was, like Wells, adjudged lbw to Ilott while Cowan removed the dangerous Darren Maddy, Stuart Law taking his third slip catch. Leicestershire were now 31 for 6.

Ronnie Irani and Stuart Law then picked up two wickets apiece as the County Champions elect crumbled to 76 all out in the 28th over to leave Essex the victors by a margin of 192 runs.

Essex captain Paul Prichard not only picked up the Benson and Hedges Cup but also the Gold Award for a commanding innings of 92 from 113 balls.

GOLD AWARD WINNER 1998
PAUL PRICHARD

This Billericay-born batsman had an excellent first season with Essex in 1984, hitting 888 runs at an average of 32.88 and scoring his maiden first-class century against Lancashire at Old Trafford. There followed

another highly promising season before he topped the 1,000-run mark in 1986 and made a highest score of 147 not out against Nottinghamshire at Chelmsford. That summer Essex won the County Championship and there is no doubt that Prichard benefited greatly from Allan Border's presence both on and off the field.

Injuries restricted his appearances in 1987 but the following summer in spite of not reaching three figures, he again topped the 1,000-run mark. After a disappointing 1989, he bounced back to form in 1990, scoring 1,276 runs at an average of 47.25 and hitting the highest score of his career – 245 against Leicestershire at Chelmsford – sharing in a new Essex record stand of 403 for the second wicket with Graham Gooch.

He maintained his form the following season, scoring 1,031 runs at 36.82 as Essex won the County Championship, and then again in 1992 he scored 1,399 runs at 43.71 as the county won the title for a second successive year. Despite a disappointing finish in the County Championship in 1993, Prichard again scored freely, including another double hundred – 225 against Sussex at Hove.

He was appointed captain of Essex in 1995. The pressures of captaincy did not affect his batting as he continued to pass the 1,000-run mark in the 1997 season, including an innings of 224 against Kent at Canterbury. After handing over the captaincy to Nasser Hussain, injuries restricted his first team appearances but this loyal servant went on to score 16,834 first-class runs at 34.28 before parting company with the county.

BENSON AND HEDGES CUP FINAL 1998

Played at Lord's, 11 and 12 July
Toss: Leicestershire
Result: Essex won by 192 runs
Gold Award: Paul Prichard
Adjudicator: Cricket Writers' Club

ESSEX

			Fall of Wickets		
P.J. Prichard	c Simmons b Williamson	92	1st	40
S.G. Law	c Mullally b Wells	6	2nd	174
N. Hussain	c Smith b Lewis	88	3rd	234
R.C. Irani	c Maddy b Mullally	32	4th	244
D.R.C. Law	c Lewis b Williamson	1	5th	245
A.P. Grayson	not out	9	6th	250
R.J. Rollins	c Brimson b Mullally	0	7th	265
S.D. Peters	b Mullally	9		
A.P. Cowan	not out	3		
M.C. Ilott	did not bat			
P.M. Such	did not bat			
Extras (b 2 lb 8 w 18)		28		
Total (50 overs)		**268 for 7**		

LEICESTERSHIRE

			Fall of Wickets		
D.L. Maddy	c S. Law b Cowan	5	1st	6
I.J. Sutcliffe	c S. Law b Cowan	1	2nd	6
B.F. Smith	c S. Law b Cowan	0	3rd	10
P.V. Simmons	b Ilott	2	4th	17
V.J. Wells	lbw b Ilott	1	5th	31
Aftab Habib	lbw b Ilott	5	6th	31
P.A. Nixon	not out	21	7th	36
C.C. Lewis	c Peters b Irani	0	8th	67
D. Williamson	c Hussain b S. Law	11	9th	73
A.D. Mullally	lbw b Irani	1	10th	76
M.T. Brimson	b S. Law	0		
Extras (lb 8 w 17 nb 4)		29		
Total (27.4 overs)		**76 all out**		

LEICESTERSHIRE	O	M	R	W	ESSEX	O	M	R	W
Mullally	10	1	36	3	Ilott	8	2	10	3
Lewis	9	0	59	1	Cowan	10	2	24	3
Wells	10	0	34	1	Irani	6	2	21	2
Simmons	9	0	67	0	S. Law	3.4	0	13	2
Brimson	2	0	13	0					
Williamson	10	0	49	2					

Umpires R. Julian and M.J. Kitchen

1999
GLOUCESTERSHIRE v YORKSHIRE

Gloucestershire captain Mark Alleyne batted his way into the county's cricket folklore on the grandest of all stages to end twenty-two years of suffering for Gloucestershire's loyal supporters.

Alleyne chose the Benson and Hedges Cup Final, the first major domestic confrontation of the summer, to silence the critics who doubted his side's right to be there. By the time he had departed the scene of his greatest triumph, he had hammered all Yorkshire's bowlers into submission, silenced the vociferous White Rose faithful and without doubt earned the undying respect of a fervent West Country crowd. His magnificent innings received the highest of accolades when a crowded Long Room at Lord's rose to award the Gloucestershire skipper a standing ovation. Yorkshire never really threatened Gloucestershire's 291 for 9 and were eventually dismissed for 167 in 39.5 overs.

Gloucestershire's fate was much less certain when Mark Alleyne arrived at the crease in the middle of the 17th over with their score at 75 for 2. Kim Barnett and Tim Hancock had provided the West Country side with a superb start, as they produced an enterprising opening stand of 66 in 12.5 overs. Barnett carved out 28 from 39 balls including five boundaries, while Hancock faced 51 deliveries and struck six fours in a valuable innings of 35. Once they had departed to Hutchison and White respectively, Yorkshire began to claw their way back into contention, courtesy of some fine disciplined bowling by Ryan Sidebottom and Craig White.

Kim Barnett

Craig White

It took Gloucestershire batsmen Rob Cunliffe and Alleyne several overs to find their touch, but when they did, the cricket was breathtaking! They passed the 100 landmark in the 25th over, posted their 50 partnership off just 83 balls and then reached 150 inside 35 overs.

Cunliffe matched his skipper blow for blow and reached his half-century off 71 balls. Alleyne also posted his 50 in the 38th over as this third wicket partnership realised 100 runs. When Cunliffe was eventually dismissed, bowled by White for 61, he had faced 81 deliveries, struck two fours and a six and helped Alleyne add 157 at a run a ball.

Alleyne continued to find the gaps, offering one chance on 88, lofting Gavin Hamilton to long-on where Paul Hutchison fumbled the catch. Yorkshire were made to pay as the Gloucestershire captain twice steered Hamilton into the Main Stand for leg-side sixes on his way to a majestic 86-ball century – the first by a Gloucestershire player at Lord's. When Craig White uprooted his off-stump in the 45th over, Alleyne had plundered 112 runs from 91 deliveries, with 11 fours and two sixes, and taken his Gloucestershire side to a position of strength at 255 for 4.

At that stage, it appeared as if Gloucestershire would set Yorkshire a total of 300 plus, but White and Hutchison managed to apply the brakes, and the latter struck a crucial blow for the White Rose county when he had Australian Ian Harvey caught in the deep by Michael Vaughan for 13. Jeremy Snape, Jack Russell, Martyn Ball and Jon Lewis all departed cheaply but Matt Windows hit an unbeaten 18 off 15 deliveries to take Gloucestershire's total to nine runs short of 300.

Requiring almost six an over, Yorkshire were always going to be up against it, even more so when Ian Harvey sent back fellow Australian Greg Blewitt, caught by Ball at first slip for nine. Yorkshire skipper David Byas then departed for 13, brilliantly caught and bowled by Dewsbury-born Mike Smith with the Yorkshire total on 45 for 2.

While Craig White remained, Yorkshire had hope but when he was bowled chasing a Jon Lewis long-hop for 38, Gloucestershire began to sense it was their day. Off-spinner Martyn Ball produced a fine delivery to bowl Michael Vaughan and then had Richard Harden caught sweeping by Cunliffe. He later knocked back Richard Blakey's off-stump to finish with 3 for 39 off his allotted ten overs.

Matt Windows had already run out Anthony McGrath with a direct hit and when Russell stumped Gavin Hamilton for 25, Yorkshire were left struggling at 163 for 8, requiring a most unlikely 10 runs per over for victory. It just remained for Snape to take a return catch off Ryan Sidebottom and Lewis to bowl Chris Silverwood before celebrations could begin.

Just as they had in 1977, West Country cricket fans rejoiced in an emphatic victory. On that Lord's occasion, it was Andy Stovold who stole the show. However, his performance was eclipsed by a knock which will be remembered for years to come by those who were privileged to witness this slaughter!

GOLD AWARD WINNER 1999
MARK ALLEYNE

A product of the Haringey Cricket School, Mark Alleyne is the youngest player in Gloucestershire's history to make a century, when he hit an unbeaten 116 against Sussex at Bristol in what was only his eighth first-class innings.

Over the next few seasons, Alleyne began to show a great maturity in his batting and in 1990, he was awarded his county cap when he finished third in the county averages with 763 runs at an average of 44.88. Included in that total was the highest score of his career, a superb 256 against Northamptonshire. The following summer saw him pass the 1,000-run mark on what was the first of six occasions – his best being 1,189 in 1998.

Appointed Gloucestershire captain in 1997, he hasn't let the pressures affect his performances and has led the county to success in both the Benson and Hedges Cup and the C&G Trophy (winners of both competitions in 1999 and 2000) and to the Division One Championship of the Norwich Union National League. His best performances on the domestic one-day front are an innings of 134 against Leicestershire in 1992 and 5 for 27 against the Combined Universities in 1988 – both matches being played at Bristol.

Alleyne, who captained England 'A' tours to New Zealand and the West Indies, has also played for England in 10 limited-overs internationals, in which his highest score was 53 against South Africa in East London, while his best bowling was 3 for 27 against Sri Lanka.

His best bowling figures of 6 for 49 against Middlesex at Lord's came in the summer of 2000, a year after being awarded a benefit and also being named as one of *Wisden*'s five 'Cricketers of the Year'.

Having just completed his seventeenth season with the county, Mark Alleyne has scored 14,512 first-class runs at an average of 31.08 and taken 394 wickets at 32.70 runs apiece.

BENSON AND HEDGES CUP FINAL 1999

Played at Lord's, 1 August
Toss: Gloucestershire
Result: Gloucestershire won by 124 runs
Gold Award: Mark Alleyne
Adjudicator: Cricket Writers' Club

GLOUCESTERSHIRE

				Fall of Wickets	
K.J. Barnett	b Hutchison	28		1st	66
T.H.C. Hancock	b White	35		2nd	75
R.J. Cunliffe	b White	61		3rd	232
M.W. Alleyne	b White	112		4th	255
I.J. Harvey	c Vaughan b Hutchison	13		5th	267
J.N. Snape	c White b Hutchison	3		6th	267
R.C. Russell	run out	1		7th	270
M.G.N. Windows	not out	18		8th	283
M.C.J. Ball	b Silverwood	2		9th	286
J. Lewis	b White	2			
A.M. Smith	not out	1			
Extras (lb 7 w 8)		15			
Total (50 overs)		**291 for 9**			

YORKSHIRE

				Fall of Wickets	
C. White	b Lewis	38		1st	14
G.S. Blewett	c Ball b Harvey	9		2nd	45
D. Byas	c and b Smith	13		3rd	78
M.P. Vaughan	b Ball	24		4th	99
A. McGrath	run out	20		5th	115
R.J. Harden	c Cunliffe b Ball	8		6th	122
G.M. Hamilton	st Russell b Lewis	25		7th	156
R.J. Blakey	b Ball	14		8th	161
C.E.W. Silverwood	b Lewis	4		9th	165
R.J. Sidebottom	c and b Snape	0		10th	167
P.M. Hutchison	not out	2			
Extras (b 1 lb 5 w 4)		10			
Total (40 overs)		**167 all out**			

YORKSHIRE	O	M	R	W	GLOUCESTERSHIRE	O	M	R	W
Silverwood	10	0	47	1	Smith	8	0	28	1
Hamilton	6	0	55	0	Harvey	5	0	25	1
Hutchison	5	0	30	3	Lewis	5	0	32	3
Sidebottom	10	0	54	0	Alleyne	6	1	17	0
White	10	0	51	4	Ball	10	1	39	3
Vaughan	6	0	24	0	Snape	6	0	20	1
Blewitt	3	0	23	0					

Umpires R. Julian and P. Willey

2000
GLAMORGAN v GLOUCESTERSHIRE

Australian Ian Harvey swept Gloucestershire into cricketing folklore at a sun-drenched Lord's in 2000. Certainly no man did more to ensure a record third successive cup final triumph as Gloucestershire overhauled Glamorgan's total of 225 with seven wickets and more than three overs in hand.

Harvey's outstanding array of slower balls and yorkers saw him join Steve Jefferies of Hampshire and Joel Garner of Somerset in a select band of players to have taken five wickets in a Benson and Hedges Cup Final. His 5 for 34 in 9.3 overs not only helped to nullify Matthew Maynard's excellent century but also provided the platform from which Gloucestershire's batsmen were able to launch their victory charge.

The Australian exploited early movement to remove both of the Glamorgan openers – Robert Croft and fellow Australian Matthew Elliott – in the space of ten balls to leave the Welsh county 24 for 2. A baffled Croft, who had just been recalled to the England Test side for the opening battle with the West Indies at Edgbaston, lofted a catch to mid-off which was brilliantly held by Jon Lewis, while Elliott was beaten for movement and bowled off an inside edge.

It was then that Glamorgan captain Matthew Maynard and Mike Powell set about repairing the damage, hoping to repeat their feat of the semi-final victory over Surrey by turning a shaky start into a platform from which a challenging score could be posted.

Robert Croft

Matthew Maynard was making his first appearance in a Lord's final at the age of 34 but he was in his element in stroking his way to 104 from only 118 balls. His innings followed a match-winning 109 in the semi-final. It was an innings reminiscent of previous centuries scored in the final, perhaps notably those scored by Graham Gooch, Aravinda de Silva and the great Viv Richards.

But Mike Powell spent 97 balls in compiling 48 runs, while the in-form Maynard was crucially kept away from the strike. In fact, in the final ten overs, when Glamorgan should have been looking to accelerate, the Glamorgan leader faced only 23 balls! The two batsmen had added 137 for the third wicket when Powell misjudged a drive to give a return catch to Jeremy Snape.

Matthew Maynard

The fall of this wicket sparked a collapse which saw Glamorgan lose eight wickets in just nine-and-a-half overs and fall at least 25 runs short of what would have been a challenging total. Maynard was certainly let down by his team-mates as he watched six partners dismissed in a bewildering exhibition of ill-advised stroke play and poor decision-making. Adrian Dale was run out going for a non-existent single but the other five wickets belonged to Ian Harvey and the fast emerging James Averis, who bowled intelligently at the death to pick up the wickets of Steve James and Adrian Shaw.

Gloucestershire's batting possessed too great a depth to allow a winning position to slip away and following a succession of friendly half-volleys, Hancock and Barnett kept the cover drives flowing to give Gloucestershire a fine start. Gloucestershire's openers had put on 80 for the first wicket when Kim Barnett chased a wide delivery from Croft and dragged the ball onto his stumps in the 20th over. The veteran opener, playing in his fourth consecutive Lord's final and his seventh in all, contributed 39 to overhaul Middlesex's Mike Gatting as the second highest run-scorer in the history of the Benson and Hedges Cup.

Rob Cunliffe joined Hancock and played some fine strokes as he demonstrated his speed between the wickets in scoring a quickfire 24 from 40 balls before gloving a fast-rising delivery from Steve Watkin to Shaw. Tim Hancock had moved on to 60 when he offered a difficult return catch to Glamorgan youngster Owen Parkin – Gloucestershire 131 for 3.

But the West Country side were not to be denied and Matt Windows and captain Mark Alleyne combined to add 95 runs in an unbroken fourth-wicket stand which carried Gloucestershire to victory well ahead of schedule. Windows cracked eight boundaries in a superb 59-ball 53 which confirmed his reputation as one of the best back-foot players on the county circuit. Though he had failed to impress the watching England selectors with the ball, Mark Alleyne demonstrated a West Indian flamboyance in making an unbeaten 40 including the winning run in the 47th over.

Gloucestershire's status as the new kings of one-day cricket in England and one of the most successful sides in the history of the game was reaffirmed.

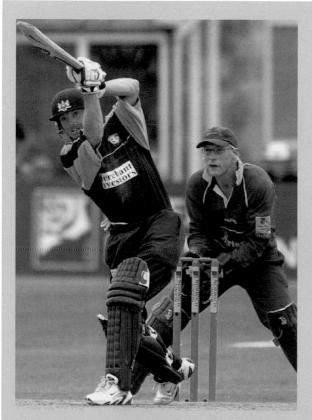

GOLD AWARD WINNER 2000
IAN HARVEY

Ian Harvey has played a major role in Gloucestershire's one-day successes.

Playing for Victoria since 1993–94, the Australian all-rounder's best performances with the bat and ball have both come against South Australia in matches at Melbourne. During the course of the 1995–96 season, he hit 136 and the following season took 7 for 44 to help Victoria to two important wins. It was performances like this that led to him making his one-day international debut for Australia against South Africa at Sydney in the Carlton Series of 1997–98.

Harvey, who has played in thirty-eight limited-over internationals for Australia, has a highest score of 47 not out against the West Indies at Sydney and best bowling figures of 4 for 28 against Zimbabwe at Melbourne, both during the 2001–02 season. Also that summer, while playing for Victoria, he performed the hat-trick.

Harvey is a one-day expert who provides impetus to the middle-order with his attacking stroke play; he also possesses a bowling style that has on occasions, made him lethal in English conditions. He conjures up a skidding bounce which, allied to a deceptive slower ball, makes batting against him extremely hazardous towards the end of an innings. However, he is a victim of Australia's wealth of talent, forever living on the fringe of international duty.

Though undoubtedly a one-day specialist, he has scored 4,761 first-class runs with a best of 130 against Middlesex at Lord's in 2001 and captured 278 wickets with a best for Gloucestershire of 6 for 19 (10 for 32 in the match) against Sussex at Hove a year earlier.

BENSON AND HEDGES CUP FINAL 2000

Played at Lord's, 10 June
Toss: Gloucestershire
Result: Gloucestershire won by seven wickets
Gold Award: Ian Harvey
Adjudicator: Cricket Writers' Club

GLAMORGAN

				Fall of Wickets	
R.D.B. Croft	c Lewis b Harvey	11		1st	18
M.T.G. Elliott	b Harvey	9		2nd	24
M.J. Powell	c and b Snape	48		3rd	161
M.P. Maynard	run out	104		4th	178
A. Dale	run out	5		5th	192
S.P. James	b Averis	7		6th	195
K. Newell	c Cunliffe b Harvey	1		7th	202
A.D. Shaw	c Barnett b Averis	1		8th	213
A.G. Wharf	lbw b Harvey	8		9th	225
S.L. Watkin	b Harvey	10		10th	225
O.T. Parkin	not out	0			
Extras (lb 5 w 8 nb 8)		21			
Total (49.3 overs)		**225 all out**			

GLOUCESTERSHIRE

				Fall of Wickets	
T.H.C. Hancock	c and b Parkin	60		1st	80
K.J. Barnett	b Croft	39		2nd	118
R.J. Cunliffe	c Shaw b Watkin	24		3rd	131
M.G.N. Windows	not out	53			
M.W. Alleyne	not out	40			
I.J. Harvey	did not bat				
R.C. Russell	did not bat				
J.N. Snape	did not bat				
J. Averis	did not bat				
J. Lewis	did not bat				
A.M. Smith	did not bat				
Extras (b 1 lb 4 w 3 nb 2)		10			
Total (46.5 overs)		**226 for 3**			

GLOUCESTERSHIRE	O	M	R	W	GLAMORGAN	O	M	R	W
Harvey	9.3	1	34	5	Parkin	8	1	46	1
Smith	10	1	44	0	Watkin	10	1	42	1
Lewis	5	0	23	0	Wharf	10	0	48	0
Averis	10	0	49	2	Croft	10	0	39	1
Alleyne	7	0	33	0	Dale	8.5	0	46	0
Snape	8	0	37	1					

Umpires K.E. Palmer and G. Sharp

2001
GLOUCESTERSHIRE v SURREY

One-day kings Gloucestershire were dethroned at Lord's in 2001 as they failed to become the first county ever to win a hat-trick of Benson and Hedges titles. Surrey's team of international stars proved too strong as the West Country side slipped to a 47-run defeat.

Surrey captain Adam Hollioake won the toss and boldly decided to bat first beneath cloud-laden skies. He must have been having second thoughts when the previous year's hero Ian Harvey struck in only the third over of the day. He engineered a breakthrough with his seventh ball to dismiss Surrey's England opener Mark Butcher. The left-hander, who had failed to trouble the scorers, perished leg-before to a ball which cut back at him.

Surrey's top-order had blazed a trail in brushing aside Nottinghamshire in the semi-final and Ian Ward and new batsman Mark Ramprakash began to put bat to ball. The England pair fed voraciously on a series of over-pitched deliveries from James Averis, who conceded 18 runs

Mark Ramprakash

Jack Russell

from his first couple of overs. Surrey were off to a flying start – Ramprakash cut and pulled his way to 39 off just 33 balls, helping Ward add 64 at a run a ball before suffering a rush of blood. Alleyne, who had gone for 13 off his first over, had his revenge when the former Middlesex batsman tried to lift him for six over square-leg but only succeeded in finding Chris Taylor on the boundary.

Ward continued to play second fiddle, allowing Surrey's stroke-makers to play their shots. But Mark Alleyne had other ideas and dismissed Alec Stewart and Alistair Brown in quick succession. Both departed to poor shots as Surrey slipped to 97 for 4 inside 20 overs. Alec Stewart was hurried up by a sharp delivery which he scooped to Jeremy Snape at mid-off, while Brown edged to Harvey at slip. Though the England wicket-keeper had only scored eight runs, his innings was notable for a heated discussion with Alleyne after Dominic Hewson's throw had hit Ward on the helmet. Umpires Ken Palmer and John Hampshire had to intervene to calm the situation. Alleyne had taken 3 for 25 in five overs to peg Surrey back.

Ward had been batting well but soon after this incident, he departed for an impressive 54 from just 59 deliveries, as he flayed outside off-stump and was snapped up by Russell to present Mark Hardinges with a wicket from only his second ball. The Surrey opener was the fifth man out with the score on 118.

Ben Hollioake walked out to join his elder brother and the two of them rebuilt the innings with a superb stand of 84. They began by scampering quick singles and picking the gaps well. It was Ben Hollioake who took on the role of the aggressor, crashing a leg-side six off Alleyne, as the Gloucestershire skipper went for 15 in his final over, and another mighty six over mid-wicket off Hardinges.

The partnership was finally broken when Adam Hollioake tried to reverse sweep a straight delivery from Ball which thudded into his pads and gave umpire Palmer an easy decision. The Gloucestershire spinner then had Tudor leg-before to leave Surrey on 204 for 7. Martin Bicknell joined the younger Hollioake and though he rode his luck, notably when Taylor allowed a catch to slip through his hands on the deep square-leg boundary for six, he helped add 38 runs off 34 balls for the eighth wicket. Hollioake eventually departed in the penultimate over, having scored a brilliant 73 at a run a ball.

In the absence of opener Tim Hancock, who had broken his hand, Jack Russell was pushed up the order to open with Barnett. Deprived of room outside the off-stump, Barnett took 19 balls to get off the mark and then had his off-stump knocked back by Giddins with 35 on the board. Adam Hollioake then introduced the wiles of Pakistani leg-spinner Saqlain into the attack and he soon forced Hewson to hole out to Bicknell at mid-off. Giddins picked up another couple of wickets as the former Sussex bowler exerted lateral moment to send back Harvey and Windows.

Russell, though, was playing well and he reached his half-century from 84 balls. Alleyne seemed prepared to play his shots and he hit Ben Hollioake back over his head for six. He and Russell had added 42 for the fifth wicket when Tudor tucked up the Gloucestershire wicket-keeper and he gave a catch to his opposite number. Russell's departure caused an alarming slide. Alleyne lobbed a full toss back to Saqlain, having scored 26 from 32 balls. The Surrey leg-spinner then bowled Taylor before Tudor found the edge of Snape's bat. Hardinges gave Bicknell his only success before last man James Averis was bowled by Tudor, who finished with 3 for 28 to bring down the curtain on perhaps the most incredible run of success in the history of English one-day cricket.

BENSON AND HEDGES CUP FINAL 2001

Played at Lord's, 14 July
Toss: Surrey
Result: Surrey won by 47 runs
Gold Award: Ben Hollioake
Adjudicator: Cricket Writers' Club

SURREY

			Fall of Wickets	
M.A. Butcher	lbw b Harvey	0	1st	7
I.J. Ward	c Russell b Hardinges	54	2nd	71
M.R. Ramprakash	c Taylor b Alleyne	39	3rd	89
A.J. Stewart	c Snape b Alleyne	8	4th	97
A.D. Brown	c Harvey b Alleyne	3	5th	118
A.J. Hollioake	lbw b Ball	39	6th	202
B.C. Hollioake	c Alleyne b Averis	73	7th	204
A.J. Tudor	lbw b Ball	1	8th	242
M.P. Bicknell	b Harvey	19	9th	244
Saqlain Mushtaq	not out	1	10th	244
E.S.H. Giddins	b Harvey	0		
Extras (lb 4 w 3)		7		
Total (49.5 overs)		**244 all out**		

GLOUCESTERSHIRE

			Fall of Wickets	
R.C. Russell	c Stewart b Tudor	62	1st	35
K.J. Barnett	b Giddins	7	2nd	68
D.R. Hewson	c Bicknell b Saqlain Mushtaq	11	3rd	71
I.J. Harvey	lbw b Giddins	1	4th	89
M.G.N. Windows	b Giddins	10	5th	131
M.W. Alleyne	c and b Saqlain Mushtaq	26	6th	133
J.N. Snape	c Stewart b Tudor	22	7th	161
C.G. Taylor	b Saqlain Mushtaq	12	8th	190
M.A. Hardinges	c Stewart b Bicknell	12	9th	194
M.C.J. Ball	not out	3	10th	197
J.M.M. Averis	b Tudor	1		
Extras (lb 16 w 14)		30		
Total (45.5 overs)		**197 all out**		

GLOUCESTERSHIRE	O	M	R	W
Harvey	9.5	2	43	3
Averis	10	1	65	1
Alleyne	10	1	51	3
Ball	10	0	39	2
Hardinges	7	0	31	1
Barnett	3	0	11	0

SURREY	O	M	R	W
Bicknell	10	1	38	1
Tudor	9.5	3	28	3
Giddins	8	1	31	3
Saqlain Mushtaq	8	0	37	3
B. Hollioake	10	0	47	0

Umpires J.H. Hampshire and K.E. Palmer

2002

ESSEX v WARWICKSHIRE

This wasn't quite the send off that Lord's had in mind for the last Benson and Hedges Cup Final. Warwickshire played well to lift the trophy, but Essex's failings meant that a near sell-out crowd missed out on a game they had hoped would live up to the great Lord's showpieces of the past.

Essex had enjoyed a fine season up to the final, but Graham Gooch's rejuvenated side failed to make the most of a blameless pitch. A target of 182 was certainly well below par and despite a late stutter Warwickshire passed the total with 13.4 overs to spare to record a five-wicket win.

As Dougie Brown pulled Graham Napier through mid-wicket for the winning runs and celebrated wildly, Gold Award winner Ian Bell calmly shook hands with the opposition. Unbeaten on 65, the Warwickshire No. 3 had top-scored again after doing so in the quarter-final and semi-final victories.

Essex made a disastrous start when England captain Nasser Hussain got an edge to the second ball of the match from Shaun Pollock and Keith Piper took the catch. This set a disciplined tone for Warwickshire's bowling which resulted in the dismissal of Graham Napier. Refused a third run by Robinson, he was run out by a direct hit from Jim Troughton on the mid-wicket boundary after consultation with the third umpire. If Napier's fate was bad, John Stephenson's was worse. He was dismissed first ball, dragging on a delivery from Neil Carter to collect his fourth duck of the summer's Benson and Hedges competition. Darren Robinson then departed to a wholly over-ambitious shot off Carter and was caught by Brown to leave Essex 40 for 4 off 10 overs.

Essex skipper Ronnie Irani could not work the ball around and, frustrated, got himself out as soon as he went aerial, lofting Dougie Brown to Neil Smith. It was Neil Smith who dismissed the second of Essex's big guns, having Zimbabwean Test player Andy Flower caught down the leg-side by Keith Piper. Standing up, it was a fine catch by the Warwickshire wicket-keeper.

The lower order scraped about to provide a target as Paul Grayson added 47 off 48 balls with Ashley Cowan, but when the Essex paceman hit Smith for four in the last over, it was Essex's first boundary for 27 overs.

When Warwickshire's openers, captain Michael Powell and Test star Nick Knight, both fell to loose drives with just 21 on the board, Essex were back with a sniff and something to bowl at. This was the cue for two young batsmen – Ian Bell and Jim Troughton – to come together to lift the occasion and give the crowd some batting to remember.

For a couple of overs, they played themselves in and steadied the innings. Bell and the left-handed Troughton certainly had their luck, Bell surviving a close lbw call to Irani on nought as well as inside-edging Andy Clarke, and Troughton slicing a few of his drives after advancing down the pitch.

Ronnie Irani

Troughton got off the mark by smashing Irani for four and followed it with two more boundaries off the next two deliveries. Bell joined in with strokes all round the wicket. After getting their eye in, he and Troughton took 41 off four overs of medium pace. Their 50 stand was the first of the game and, all in all, they added 84 from 72 balls in taking the game away from Essex. When Troughton was caught skying to mid-on, Shaun Pollock kept the momentum going, making 34 from 31 balls, until the outcome was virtually sealed.

Ian Bell produced a technically flawless innings, driving well on both sides of the wicket and working the singles intelligently. Named 'Man of the Match' by the former captains of the counties who had won this competition, he shaped his game to be a sensible complement, pushing the ball around and taking 24 singles in his innings, along with seven boundaries.

Ronnie Irani, the Essex captain, had the satisfaction of breaking the record for the most wickets in a Benson and Hedges season with 20 but this was little comfort: as his side lost with 14 overs to spare!

So the Benson and Hedges Cup came to an end, to be replaced by a 20-over competition. Certainly in the 1970s, and perhaps in the 1980s, the summer calendar had the scope for two domestic cup finals but not now, following the expansion of England's international programme.

A fourth competition, which is what the Benson and Hedges Cup was, arguably led to a further dilution of the intensity of county cricket and of England's Test team. There is no doubt, however, that the Benson and Hedges Cup, with its thirty-one years of loyal support, represented a major stage for cricket.

GOLD AWARD WINNER 2002
IAN BELL

Ian Bell was introduced to cricket at Dunchurch, his local village club, but it was at Coventry and North Warwicks, a progressive Birmingham League club, that he was spotted by Warwickshire. He was fast-tracked through the county's youth system and though he might have forged a career in rugby or football, being fly-half for Rugby Lions' junior teams and a good enough right-back to secure a place at Coventry City's

School of Excellence, he opted for cricket.

The Warwickshire batting prodigy has grown accustomed to having praise showered on him since he made his first England Under 19 tour as a raw 16-year-old. When he returned home from that tour of New Zealand, he decided cricket would take precedence but that he would also continue with his studies. It was while he was at Princethorpe College near Leamington that Bell, then 17 years old, was summoned to make his first-class debut against Sussex in the final Championship match of 1999. It was quite an inauspicious start as he was bowled by Jason Lewry for a duck!

Exams and England Under 19 commitments restricted his availability in the summer of 2000 but the following year he finished ninth in the national averages with 836 runs from 16 innings, including three centuries and two scores of 98. The runs, which included 571 in his last seven innings, were scored with a sound but simple technique, mature shot selection and an unflappable temperament.

He was an automatic choice for the first intake of players for the National Academy since, like all good players, he plays the ball late, and when he's really on form he plays it from right under his eyes. In 2002 he scored 658 runs at 24.37 and of course won the Gold Award in the very last Benson and Hedges Final.

The England management were doubtless right when they decided that Bell was better off playing county cricket for a little while longer before taking the step to international level. However, it is a shame that the 20-year-old has not yet been blooded: when he is, the going may be tougher than it was in the summer of 2002.

BENSON AND HEDGES CUP FINAL 2002

Played at Lord's, 22 June
Toss: Warwickshire
Result: Warwickshire won by five wickets
Gold Award: Ian Bell
Adjudicator: Previous winning captains

ESSEX

			Fall of Wickets	
N. Hussain	c Piper b Pollock	0	1st	0
D.D.J. Robinson	c Brown b Carter	18	2nd	33
G.R. Napier	run out	17	3rd	33
J.P. Stephenson	b Carter	0	4th	40
A. Flower	c Piper b Smith	30	5th	61
R.C. Irani	c Smith b Brown	8	6th	86
A. Habib	c Knight b Giles	19	7th	109
A.P. Grayson	not out	38	8th	134
J.M. Dakin	c Powell b Brown	12		
A.P. Cowan	not out	27		
A.J. Clarke	did not bat			
Extras (lb 4 w 4 nb 4)		12		
Total (50 overs)		**181 for 8**		

WARWICKSHIRE

			Fall of Wickets	
M.J. Powell	c Flower b Cowan	11	1st	19
N.V. Knight	c Flower b Irani	9	2nd	21
I.R. Bell	not out	65	3rd	105
J.O. Troughton	c Flower b Napier	37	4th	158
S.M. Pollock	c Dakin b Irani	34	5th	159
T.L. Penney	lbw b Stephenson	0		
D.R. Brown	not out	12		
N.M.K. Smith	did not bat			
A.F. Giles	did not bat			
K.J. Piper	did not bat			
N.M. Carter	did not bat			
Extras (lb 6 w 8)		14		
Total (36.2 overs)		**182 for 5**		

WARWICKSHIRE

	O	M	R	W
Pollock	10	1	32	1
Carter	10	1	45	2
Brown	10	0	32	2
Giles	10	1	28	1
Smith	10	0	40	1

ESSEX

	O	M	R	W
Irani	10	2	40	2
Cowan	8	0	37	1
Clarke	2	0	20	0
Dakin	2	0	22	0
Grayson	4	0	11	0
Napier	5.2	0	31	1
Stephenson	5	0	15	1

Umpires B.D. Dudleston and J.H. Hampshire

PRINCIPAL COMPETITION RECORDS 1972-2002

Highest Total	388 for 7	Essex v Scotland at Chelmsford 1992
Highest Total (Batting Second)	318 for 5	Lancashire v Leicestershire at Old Trafford 1995
Lowest Total	50	Hampshire v Yorkshire at Headingley 1991
Highest Score	198*	G.A. Gooch (Essex v Sussex) at Hove 1982
Fastest Hundred	62 min	M.A. Nash (Glamorgan v Hampshire) at Swansea 1976

Highest partnerships for each wicket

1st	252	V.P. Terry/C.L. Smith	Hampshire v Combined Universities at Southampton 1990
2nd	285*	C.G. Greenidge/D.R. Turner	Hampshire v Minor Counties (S) at Amersham 1973
3rd	271	C.J. Adams/M.G. Bevan	Sussex v Essex at Chelmsford 2000
4th	207	R.C. Russell/A.J. Wright	Gloucestershire v British Universities at Bristol 1998
5th	160	A.J. Lamb/D.J. Capel	Northants v Leicestershire at Northampton 1986
6th	167*	M.G. Bevan/R.J. Blakey	Yorkshire v Lancashire at Old Trafford 1996
7th	149*	J.D. Love/C.M. Old	Yorkshire v Scotland at Bradford 1981
8th	109	R.E. East/N. Smith	Essex v Northants at Chelmsford 1977
9th	83	P.G. Newman/M.A. Holding	Derbyshire v Notts at Trent Bridge 1985
10th	80*	D.L. Bairstow/C.M. Johnson	Yorkshire v Derbyshire at Derby 1981

Best bowling

7 for 12	W.W. Daniel	Middlesex v Minor Counties (S) at Ipswich 1978
7 for 22	J.R. Thomson	Middlesex v Hampshire at Lord's 1981
7 for 24	Mushtaq Ahmed	Somerset v Ireland at Taunton 1997
7 for 32	R.G.D. Willis	Warwickshire v Leicestershire at Edgbaston 1981

Four wickets in four balls

S. Pollock	Warwickshire v Leicestershire at Edgbaston 1996

Most wicket-keeping dismissals in an innings

D.J.S. Taylor	8 (8 ct)	Somerset v Combined Universities at Taunton 1982

Most catches in an innings

V.J. Marks	5	Combined Universities v Kent at Oxford 1976

Benson and Hedges Cup Finals

Winners

1972	Leicestershire	1983	Middlesex	1994	Warwickshire
1973	Kent	1984	Lancashire	1995	Lancashire
1974	Surrey	1985	Leicestershire	1996	Lancashire
1975	Leicestershire	1986	Middlesex	1997	Surrey
1976	Kent	1987	Yorkshire	1998	Essex
1977	Gloucestershire	1988	Hampshire	1999	Gloucestershire
1978	Kent	1989	Nottinghamshire	2000	Gloucestershire
1979	Essex	1990	Lancashire	2001	Surrey
1980	Northamptonshire	1991	Worcestershire	2002	Warwickshire
1981	Somerset	1992	Hampshire		
1982	Somerset	1993	Derbyshire		

Highest totals

291 for 9	(50 overs)	Gloucestershire v Yorkshire 1999
290 for 6	(55 overs)	Essex v Surrey 1979
274 for 7	(55 overs)	Lancashire v Kent 1995
268 for 7	(50 overs)	Essex v Leicestershire 1998
255	(51.4 overs)	Surrey v Essex 1979

Lowest totals

76	(27.4 overs)	Leicestershire v Essex 1998
117	(46.3 overs)	Derbyshire v Hampshire 1988
130	(50.1 overs)	Nottinghamshire v Somerset 1982
136 for 9	(55 overs)	Yorkshire v Leicestershire 1972
139	(50.4 overs)	Warwickshire v Lancashire 1984

Hundreds in a final

132*	I.V.A. Richards	Somerset v Surrey 1981
120	G.A. Gooch	Essex v Surrey 1979
112	P.A. de Silva	Kent v Lancashire 1995
112	M.W. Alleyne	Gloucestershire v Yorkshire 1999
104	M.P. Maynard	Glamorgan v Gloucestershire 2000